T5-AGQ-020

G. L. Smith

PAPERS
OF THE
PEABODY MUSEUM OF ARCHAEOLOGY AND
ETHNOLOGY, HARVARD UNIVERSITY
VOL. 64, NO. 3

THE ALTAR DE SACRIFICIOS EXCAVATIONS

GENERAL SUMMARY AND CONCLUSIONS

BY

GORDON R. WILLEY

PUBLISHED BY THE PEABODY MUSEUM
CAMBRIDGE, MASSACHUSETTS, U.S.A.
1973

A current list of all publications available can be obtained by writing to the
Publications Department
Peabody Museum
Harvard University
11 Divinity Avenue
Cambridge, Massachusetts 02138

THE ALTAR DE SACRIFICIOS EXCAVATIONS

GENERAL SUMMARY AND CONCLUSIONS

PAPERS
OF THE
PEABODY MUSEUM OF ARCHAEOLOGY AND
ETHNOLOGY, HARVARD UNIVERSITY
VOL. 64, NO. 3

THE ALTAR DE SACRIFICIOS EXCAVATIONS

GENERAL SUMMARY AND CONCLUSIONS

BY

GORDON R. WILLEY

PUBLISHED BY THE PEABODY MUSEUM
CAMBRIDGE, MASSACHUSETTS, U.S.A.
1973

ISBN 0-87365-185-5
LIBRARY OF CONGRESS CATALOG CARD NUMBER 73-77202
PRINTED BY THE CRIMSON PRINTING COMPANY
CAMBRIDGE, MASSACHUSETTS, U.S.A.

PREFACE

This is the final number of the Altar de Sacrificios papers as released in the Papers of the Peabody Museum, Harvard University. These monographs have been published in three volumes:

Vol. 62, No. 1. *The Ruins of Altar de Sacrificios, Department of Peten, Guatemala: An Introduction.* By Gordon R. Willey and A. Ledyard Smith. 1969.

No. 2. *Excavations at Altar de Sacrificios: Architecture, Settlement, Burials, and Caches.* By A. Ledyard Smith. 1972.

Vol. 63, No. 1. *The Ceramics of Altar de Sacrificios.* By Richard E. W. Adams. 1971.

No. 2. *The Human Skeletal Remains of Altar de Sacrificios: An Osteobiographic Analysis.* By Frank P. Saul. 1972.

Vol. 64, No. 1. *The Artifacts of Altar de Sacrificios.* By Gordon R. Willey. 1972.

No. 2. *The Hieroglyphic Inscriptions and Monumental Art of Altar de Sacrificios.* By John A. Graham. 1972.

No. 3. *The Altar de Sacrificios Excavations: General Summary and Conclusions.* By Gordon R. Willey. (The present paper.) 1973.

We have issued these results of the Altar de Sacrificios investigations as a series of separate papers for two reasons. First, by doing this it was possible to make parts of the story available earlier than if we had waited until all of the component sections had been completed. Second, by bringing the monographs out individually we can provide the more specialized reader (who may be interested only in hieroglyphics or physical anthropology, for example) with what he wants without making it necessary for him to obtain all of the Altar de Sacrificios reports. On the negative side, the separate publication of the several topics has necessitated a certain amount of repetition in the introductory material in each, and it has made for some disjunctions in what could have been a more even flow of presentation. We have tried, however, to keep such introductory statements to minimal lengths, and one of the purposes of this summary of the several Altar monographs is to explain or reconcile any apparent contradictions or disjunctions among them.

For those who are interested in reading all of the Altar de Sacrificios reports, we suggest beginning with the *Introduction* (vol. 62, no. 1), followed by the *Excavations* (vol. 62, no. 2). The four monographs on *Ceramics* (vol. 63, no. 1), *Human Skeletal Remains* (vol. 63, no. 2), *Artifacts* (vol. 64, no. 1), and *Hieroglyphic Inscriptions and Monumental Art* (vol. 64, no. 2) may then be read in any order desired, to be followed, finally, by this present paper.

This *General Summary and Conclusions* opens with a section entitled "Recapitulation," which is just that. It repeats, in very summary fashion, what has been said in our introductory paper to the Altar de Sacrificios series, plus some selected information from the other monographs. It is designed for a reader who is interested only in a relatively general statement on the Altar de Sacrificios work and who probably will not read any of the other monographs except this one. For the student with more specialized research interests who has read the preceding papers of the series, it can be omitted. The "Recapitulation" is followed by the long section on "Culture-Historical Integration," which is the main body of this summary. It opens with a consideration of phase definitions, of relative and absolute chronology, and with an explanation of some of the difficulties and problems confronted.

This is followed with a phase by phase descriptive historical reconstruction of Altar de Sacrificios throughout the span of its pre-Columbian occupance. Data are integrated into a series of individual functioning cultures and also into the wider contexts of southern Maya lowland culture as a whole. "Comments on Ethnohistory and Archaeology" is concerned with attempts at ethnic identifications of archaeological peoples and events and deals, specifically, with the possible role of the Chontal or Putun Maya in Late Classic and Early Postclassic times. The section headed "Trends" views the pre-Columbian occupance of Altar de Sacrificios through time. That is, it is the diachronic counterpart of the synchronic presentations offered in "Culture-Historical Integration." In it we are inspecting the record for change through time, for continuities or discontinuities, for increasing or decreasing emphases in all of the various aspects of the cultural record, and for the covariances in this record which may point us toward the understanding of processes. "Closing Comment on Initial Problems" is a quick retrospective look at the problems we had in mind at the outset of the Altar de Sacrificios excavations and what we have done about them. Finally, "Toward Process" is a trial run at the elucidation of process or cause in some aspects of the culture change seen in the trends at Altar de Sacrificios.

The *General Summary and Conclusions* is, obviously, based primarily upon the other monographs of the series which have preceded it. While we will make specific reference to them from time to time, we will not do this in every instance in which they are involved; that is, they are to be taken for granted as the sources upon which I have drawn. Each of these monographs has, in turn, an extensive bibliography. In some cases, we will repeat these citations, and the full references are given in the bibliography here; however, I have made no attempt to be thorough and exhaustive about this for the interested reader may consult the particular Altar de Sacrificios monograph in question for full bibliographic enlightenment. For especially controversial points or for data and opinions that are introduced into this Altar series for the first time, I will give, of course, appropriate citations.

In preparing this Summary, I have not only drawn upon the previous monographs, but I have had the benefit of consultation with and advice from my four principal collaborators, A. L. Smith, R. E. W. Adams, J. A. Graham, and Frank Saul. Each of these men has read a preliminary draft of this paper and has offered suggestions which I have followed. Each is, of course, responsible for the data which were under his charge and for many of the interpretations which have been built upon these data; however, each of these scientists has prepared his own monograph, and his part of the work should be judged essentially upon that. The way I have put all of these parts together has been largely my own responsibility.

Acknowledgment of aid and assistance given to the Altar de Sacrificios project by various persons and institutions is given in full in the introductory monograph to this series (Willey and Smith 1969). Here I would like to pay thanks to those who have helped me in the preparation of this final summary number. Barbara Westman, of the Peabody Museum staff, helped in drawing a final version of the map (fig. 1), which is based on a map originally prepared by Norman Hammond. For final manuscript typing I am indebted to my wife, Katharine W. Willey, to Maria von Mering Huggins, and to Susan Middleton. Editing of the manuscript for the printer was the work of Emily Flint and Martha Smith, under the general supervision of Burton Jones, all of the Peabody Museum Publications office.

Gordon R. Willey
Peabody Museum
Harvard University
24 October 1972

CONTENTS

FIGURES

THE ALTAR DE SACRIFICIOS EXCAVATIONS

GENERAL SUMMARY AND CONCLUSIONS

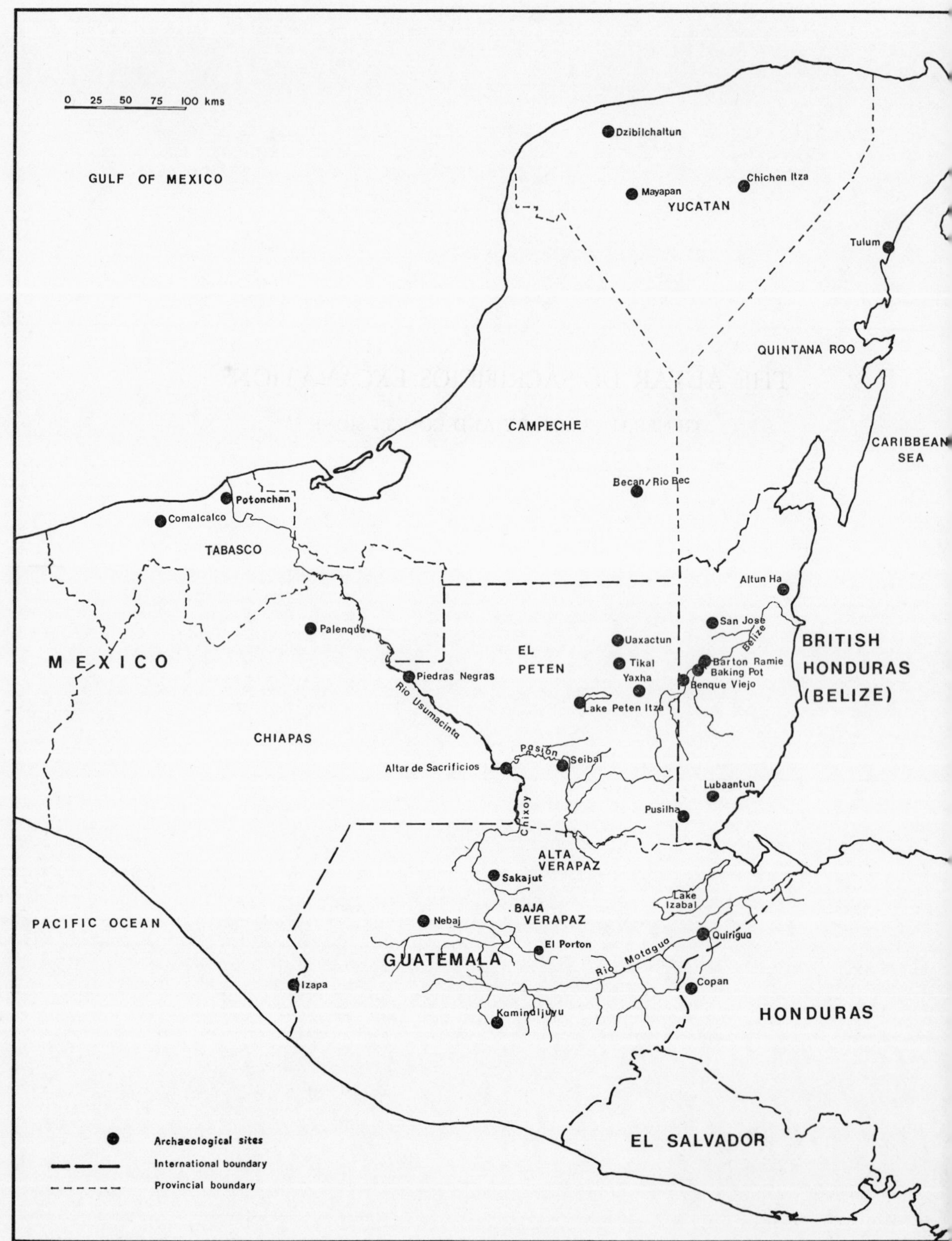

Fig. 1. Map of the Maya area showing Altar de Sacrificios and other sites mentioned in the text.

I

RECAPITULATION

THE SITE AND ITS ENVIRONS

ALTAR DE SACRIFICIOS is situated on a patch of high ground on the south bank of the Rio Pasión, just above the Rio Salinas confluence, in the southwestern portion of the Department of Peten, Guatemala (fig. 1). In the rather informal classification of Maya ruins by size, which archaeologists sometimes make, Altar is considered a "major ruin" of the southern lowlands; however, it is by no means in a class with Tikal or Yaxchilan, and it is even something less than as large as Uaxactun or Seibal. While it is not a small site, it is probably fair to say that its recognition as a major center has come from its numerous carved and dated monuments rather than from the number and size of its buildings.

Insofar as we can determine, the first published mention of Altar de Sacrificios was Maudslay's (1883), although he did not refer to it by that name. He stopped there a few hours on a day in March 1882, shortly after he had parted company with Charnay at Yaxchilan. His observations are extremely brief. He noted mounds but saw no standing buildings. He also mentioned carved stone altars.

In 1895, and again in 1904, Teobert Maler visited Altar. It was he who named the site, after a carved red sandstone altar found there. He made a sketch map, some descriptive notes, and some photographs. Subsequently, he published the first significant report on the site (Maler 1908).

Several others followed Maler, but the most important of these was Morley whose epigraphic surveys carried him there in 1914 and again in 1944. His principal publication on Altar de Sacrificios is included in his monumental *Inscriptions of Peten* (Morley 1937–38, vol. 2, pp. 309–314). This was based on his 1914 hieroglyphic notes and on a subsequent exploration and mapping of the ruins by H. E. D. Pollock, A. L. Smith, and E. M. Shook in 1937. This account of Morley's together with the 1937 map provided us with our preparatory knowledge of the site when we went there to begin the Peabody Museum work in the late 1950s.

The site is composed of three groups of large, presumably ceremonial or politico-religious structures, and a scattering of smaller mounds, or house mounds, lying immediately adjacent to the main groups. These three main groups, designated Group A, Group B, and Group C, are encompassed within a relatively small area, about 400 meters square. There are natural definitions to this site terrain. On the north is the present course of the Rio Pasión. The river has cut a steep bank here, resulting in the loss of a portion of the northernmost structures of Group A. At the south end of Group A is an ancient river course, no longer active, the Arroyo San Felix. Here the site drops off almost as sharply as on the north, and the terrain on the other side of the Arroyo San Felix is low and swampy. All along the east side of Group A the natural ground also descends abruptly into a low swale that connects, with an active stream in times of floods, the Rio Pasión with the Arroyo San Felix channel. Plazas C and B lie to the west of Plaza A Group. Here the high ground widens somewhat as it continues west, and in this direction one comes upon a number of small mounds. These continue for a distance of some 700 meters to the west of B and C Plazas. The small mounds are located on small ridges and patches of slightly higher terrain as the general ground level gradually drops off in elevation toward the Pasión-Salinas confluence, another kilometer or so still farther to the west.[1]

Prior to clearing and excavation, all of the Altar de Sacrificios mounds were covered with a combination of low bush and large trees. Only their general rectangular outlines and truncated pyramidal or platform appearance could be made out. On a cutting away of the dense vegetation the remnants of stone masonry could be seen on the larger mounds, with limestone blocks exposed on the A Group structures and red sandstone, or "redstone," on those of B and C Groups. Few of the small mounds at the western end of the site showed any surface stone. A number of stelae (mostly fallen) and altars were situated near or on the large mounds of A and B Groups. Many of these bore hieroglyphic inscriptions, as Maler had noted many years before. Potsherds were scarce on the surface of the site; however, they were found in great numbers along the riverbank where they had washed out of the big mounds at the north end of A Group.

The general environmental setting of Altar de Sacrificios is, as we have noted, the riverine lowlands of the Peten–Chiapas border. This is low-lying terrain, generally less than 400 meters above sea level, and the river channel of the lower Pasión and the Altar site is considerably below that. The underlying geological structure of the lower Pasión Valley is the karstlike limestone of the northern flanks of the Chiapas–Guatemalan highlands. There are a number of east-west anticlinal folds in this limestone, and the Rio Pasión lies in one of these. The immediate soils of the valley are of alluvial and colluvial origins; they have good nutrients, but these are lost rapidly owing to poor drainage and leaching. In agricultural potential these soils are not as good as the black rendzina-type soils that are found in some places in the Peten; however, they are better than the lateritic soils of the nearby savannas.

As far as stone resources for the ancient inhabitants of Altar de Sacrificios are concerned, limestone for the major buildings was not available in the immediate vicinity of the site. The closest deposits of which we have knowledge lie about 21 kilometers upstream on the Rio Pasión from Altar. There may have been other outcrops closer than this, but it is almost a certainty that there were none within 5 kilometers. The other major building stone of Altar, the red sandstone, is known today from outcrops along the Rio Pasión 9 kilometers upstream from the site (see A. L. Smith 1972, p. 115).[2] Some stone materials for artifactual manufacture must have been available on the lower Pasión. Flint or chert, for the making of chipped stone implements, would have occurred in nodules in the limestone beds. A black-gray conglomerate, often used for grinding implements, as well as shales and siltstones, were also probably present in the region. On the other hand, obsidians, quartzites, jadeites, diorites, and other igneous or altered igneous rocks, which are all represented in the artifact collections that we obtained at Altar, are not local but are found in the Guatemalan highlands and were probably obtained from there in ancient times.

The climate and vegetation of the lower Pasión Valley are those of a tropical rainforest. The Koeppen designation *Afw'* probably applies to the climate. There is no completely dry season although less rain falls from December to May than in the other half of the year. No exact rainfall figures are available for the immediate region, but 2000 mm or about 80 inches is a conservative annual estimate. While the vegetation along the immediate Pasión and Chixoy riverbanks is that of a tropical rainforest, to the north of the Pasión there are some sections of open savanna land. Among the big rainforest trees are mahogany (not now found on the Altar site but occurring nearby), ceiba, cedar, and guanacaste. There are a number of smaller or "second story" trees, of which the cohune or coroso palm is the most common. In general, trees are laced

1. The reader is referred to the Altar de Sacrificios site map published as figure 4 in Willey and Smith (1969) for a more exact presentation of terrain and site features.

2. See also Smith, same reference, p. 3, for the report of the geologist, Howel Williams, on the composition of this peculiar red sandstone. This Altar de Sacrificios sandstone is unique to the site; however, other local sandstones were used in other Maya sites, as at Quirigua (Graham and Williams 1971). Limestone was not the only Maya lowland building material.

with vines and lianas, and in low-lying spots, especially at Altar, there are thickets of thorny bamboo or *jimba*. The mahogany and cedar served to make large dugout canoes, in the past, certainly, as well as today. House posts and lintels were made from such trees as the zapote and cedar, or from logwood. None of these three was found growing at Altar, but they do occur elsewhere along the lower Pasión. The cohune palm, which is extremely plentiful on the site today, must have been an important ancient resource for its oil-nutritious nuts. Its leaves could also be used for roof thatch although the botan palm, not found at the site but present a few kilometers away, is a superior roofing material. The ramon tree, or breadnut, which probably provided a significant proportion of the Maya diet at some sites (Puleston and Puleston 1971) is not common at Altar or along the lower Pasión, but it does occur.[3]

Aguacates, cacao, vanilla, and tomatoes were all found in a wild state at Altar in the 1958–64 period. These may have been escapees from ancient domestication, or they may have been the original wild forms; in either case they were probably a food source for the pre-Columbian inhabitants. Other possible domesticates growing at Altar include the wiskil (huisquil), cherimoya, and guava. During our stay there our workmen grew black beans, maize, squashes, manioc, chili peppers, and sweet potatoes with great success; and it is quite likely that these were staples for the region in the past. However, some agricultural failures are worth recording. Papayas rotted and fell off the trees before they matured, and melons did not do well. This may have been due to excessive soil moisture (and bad drainage).

The lower Pasión Valley and the Peten Biotic Province lie in the Neotropica zoogeographic region although there is some overlap here with species more characteristic of the Neartica region in the north. At Altar our bone collections from the excavations, plus our own observations on living species in the region, indicated the presence of the following mammals: otter, opossum, jaguar, ocelot, peccary, deer, brocket,[4] pisote, kinkajou, tapir, bush-dog, howling monkey, spider monkey, squirrel, agouti, *gibnot*, and various bats and rodents. Similar data for birds indicated the owl, chachalaca, ocellated turkey, faisan, muscovy duck, parrots, and buzzards. The reptiles and amphibians included the crocodile, turtles, toads, frogs, the iguana, the fer-de-lance, the coral, and the boa. The most common fish in the river near Altar were the catfish or *jolote*, the blanco, and the robalo. Freshwater mussels and shrimps were also present.

THE PROBLEMS

In 1958, the year in which we decided to launch a full-scale investigation at Altar de Sacrificios, there were still relatively few major archaeological site investigations in the Maya lowlands that had been reported upon in detail. This can be said despite the fact that archaeologists probably knew more about that subarea than any other of Mesoamerica. In the southern lowlands, the territory with which we were most immediately concerned, the important sites were Uaxactun (Ricketson and Ricketson 1937, A. L. Smith 1950, R. E. Smith 1955); Holmul (Merwin and Vaillant 1932); San Jose (J. E. S. Thompson 1939); and Copan (Gordon 1896, Morley 1920, Longyear 1952). These provided the basic comparative data on architecture, ceramics, and artifacts. Uaxactun, especially, was the yardstick for ceramic typology and chronology; and it was also an important base for tying Maya cal-

3. See Willey and Smith (1969, pp. 39–47) for proper species identifications of these, as well as other flora and fauna of the region. It is to be noted that Willey and Smith state that the ramon tree is not present at Altar. According to W. R. Bullard (personal communication 1970), this is in error; a few trees do occur there.

4. Relying on earlier, tentative identifications, Willey and Smith (1969, p. 45) listed the brocket *(Mazama americana)* as being present in the Altar animal bone collections. This is an error as Olsen's (in Willey 1972) later examinations did not verify such an identification. However, the animal is to be found along the lower Pasión.

endrical dates into other aspects of the archaeological chronology. Major explorations also had been carried out at Piedras Negras (Satterthwaite 1933, 1936; Butler 1935b) and Palenque (Ruz Lhuillier 1952a, 1952b, 1958, 1962), although as of 1958 these had not yet been fully reported upon especially as regards ceramic sequences.[5] The house mound survey and stratigraphic digging of the Belize Valley had just been completed, and its results were known in a preliminary, but not yet very detailed, way (Willey et al. 1965). The very large operations at Tikal were just getting underway (Shook 1957), but this rich source of information on the ancient Maya would not be opened to students for a few years (W. R. Coe 1962, 1965).

In the northern lowlands we were mainly dependent upon the work at Chichen Itza (Morris, Charlot, and Morris 1931; Ruppert 1935) and upon some general surveys which were beginning to set up a ceramic chronology (especially Brainerd 1958). There was also some knowledge of Tulum (Lothrop 1924), not all of which had yet been published (Sanders 1960); and the major operations at Mayapan (Pollock et al. 1962) and Dzibilchaltun (Andrews IV 1960), although not yet published in final form were known in a preliminary way to workers in the Maya field.

In the Guatemalan highlands—also Maya country—the main datum point was Kaminaljuyu (Kidder, Jennings, and Shook 1946; Shook and Kidder 1952), with supplementary information coming from Zacualpa (Wauchope 1948), Nebaj (A. L. Smith and Kidder 1951), and various surveys in the highlands (Butler 1940; A. L. Smith 1955) and in the Motagua Valley (A. L. Smith and Kidder 1943).

This is not meant to be, in any way, a thorough survey of Maya archaeological research as of 1958. It overlooks such important things as Morley's (1937-38) great work on Maya hieroglyphics, Spinden's (1913) and Proskouriakoff's (1950) intersite studies of Maya sculpture and art, Thompson's (1943, 1945) articles of synthesis, and numerous other survey and lesser site reports. But to sum up, Maya archaeological knowledge as of 1958 could have been listed as something like this:

1. *Hieroglyphic-Calendric information*—Thorough, insofar as Initial Series dating was concerned, with a preponderance of opinion favoring an 11.16.0.0.0 Maya-Christian calendrical correlation.
2. *Major arts, especially sculpture*—Good descriptive knowledge, with considerable advances in chronological-developmental ordering.
3. *Architecture*—Good general descriptive knowledge of parts of the lowlands, but with major geographic gaps.
4. *Ceramic studies*—A general descriptive overview available but with fine-grained ceramic sequence information known largely from the northeastern Peten and adjacent British Honduras, Copan, and northern Yucatan. Some data from the Usumacinta and environs and some data from the Guatemalan highlands. Still many geographical gaps in the ceramic space-time framework.
5. *Settlement pattern studies*—Just beginning, with some information from the Belize Valley and Mayapan.

This itemization, which is concerned with the state of knowledge of a descriptive, spatial-temporal, primary sort alone, and which does not even venture onto more interpretive levels, gives the background for our consideration of the problems as we conceived of them in 1958. In reviewing this listing, several major geographical gaps stood out in the lowlands. One of these was in the central and southern parts of the Yucatan Peninsula, in the regions generally characterized by the Rio Bec and Chenes architectural styles.[6] Another was the little

5. This information was not to become generally available until much later. The best summary statement on ceramic sequence in the west (Usumacinta and environs) is Rands (1973). Useful survey data on the Tabasco lowlands were at hand as early as 1956 (Berlin 1956).

6. Pollock's (1970) architectural survey of Chenes ruins has since been published, and E. W. Andrews and associates began work in the Rio Bec region in the late 1960s. For a review of Maya research activities in the decade 1958–1968 see Adams (1969).

known northwestern Peten.[7] Still another was the southern Peten. And it is in this last that Altar de Sacrificios is located.

For the most part, the southern Peten, together with adjacent portions of lowland Chiapas and southern British Honduras, had known only relatively rapid archaeological survey. There had been some digging at Lubaantun[8] and Pusilha, in southern British Honduras, back in the 1920s, but the published accounts were sketchy or focused only upon specialized aspects of the work (Joyce 1926, 1933; Gruning 1930). The most adequate excavation report from the southern part of that colony was that on the minor sites of the Mountain Cow district which had been studied by Thompson (1931). In that part of Chiapas bordering the southern Peten the discovery of the famed Bonampak murals had received considerable attention (Ruppert, Thompson, and Proskouriakoff 1955), but little more was done at that site. In the Peten proper there had been no systematic explorations (other than Morley's glyphic surveys) of the southern part of that province since the very early work of Maler (1908). Neither of the two major sites of the southwestern region, Altar de Sacrificios and Seibal, had been excavated.

The decision taken in 1958 to conduct large scale and intensive excavations at Altar de Sacrificios was based primarily upon our desire to fill in a part of this southern Peten geographic gap in our knowledge of lowland Maya archaeology. Altar de Sacrificios was a major ruin in this territory. Except for Morley's epigraphic findings we knew virtually nothing about the site. These epigraphic data were, in themselves, tantalizing. The earliest recorded stelae in the southwestern Peten were at Altar. Were there other early monuments at the site? How did these stelae relate to other archaeological remains to be found there? Basic data were needed on ceramics and their sequence relationships, on other artifacts, architecture, burial practices, and on all other aspects of the archaeological culture. These data-gathering objectives were our primary research desiderata at the time we began work at Altar.

Behind this front line of research considerations there were others. These were not thought of as being secondary in importance but in order of investigation. They were essentially problems or questions of historical reconstruction. When did the first occupation of the Peten lowlands occur? And from where? By 1958 it appeared (as it still does) that the earliest farming cultures of southern Mesoamerica were to be found on the Chiapas-Guatemalan Pacific coast and adjacent highlands and in the Veracruz-Tabasco lowlands of the Mexican Gulf coast. Nothing in the Peten or Yucatan could be dated as early. The question then became, Did the earliest Maya lowland settlers—carriers of a Mamom or Mamom-like culture—come from the Guatemalan highlands or from the Olmec lowlands? Perhaps a site in the location of Altar de Sacrificios, at an important junction of rivers descending from the highlands, might throw light on this question, especially as it concerned highland-lowland relationships—or so the reasoning went.

Closely related to this was another historical concern. At its river junction location, Altar was thought of as a possible pre-Columbian Maya "crossroads" station (Willey et al. 1960). Upstream on the Pasión and Salinas-Chixoy were a large portion of the southern Peten lowlands and the highlands of the Guatemalan Baja Verapaz and Alta Verapaz; downstream, below the Pasión-Salinas juncture, the Salinas was joined by the Lacantun-Lacanja to become the Usumacinta system, leading on to the regions of Yaxchilan, Piedras Negras, Palenque, and the Gulf coast. In our attempt to correlate Maya lowland regional sequences, as well as those of the highlands, it was thought that Altar de Sacrificios might provide a strategic point of overlap.

In this connection of Altar de Sacrificios as a crossroads, the matter of pre-Columbian trade was also seen as a subsidiary line of research; however, it is fair to say that this "trade" problem did not loom as large in

7. A region since explored, in a preliminary way, by Ian Graham (personal communication 1964–1972), of the Peabody Museum staff, in connection with his hieroglyphic survey.

8. Since excavated in a more systematic way by Norman Hammond (1970).

American archaeological thinking in the late 1950s and early 1960s as it did later. Trade items were appreciated more as elements indicative of intercultural and interregional contacts, with an eye to cross-dating, and less as clues to the nature and functioning of the institution of trade itself. No hypotheses about the systemic role of trade within Maya culture, such as those developed more recently by Rathje (1971a and b), motivated us at that time. We were, however, concerned and curious about the river-junction location of the site. This location suggested trading or military functions, or both, functions of the location that would have outweighed the disadvantages of swamplike setting and lack of stone and of certain wood resources.

Another problem with which we were concerned in 1958 was that of Mexican relationships with the Maya. Essentially historical in nature, at least as we conceived of it then, it also had important functional-developmental implications. As Altar de Sacrificios lay near the western edge of the Maya lowlands—the side closest to central Mexico—it was speculated that we might pick up strong Teotihuacan evidences here and gain more precise knowledge of their chronology and their effects upon the Maya. This was before the Tikal excavations had revealed the pattern of a Teotihuacan trait concentration at that site, derived, probably, by way of Kaminaljuyu, and from there an apparent spread of these traits to other southern Maya lowland sites. Thus, while we did find Teotihuacanoid elements at Altar and could pin down their appearance within fairly fine-scale chronological limits, we did not discover Altar to have been especially exposed to Teotihuacan influence.

In addition to the question of Teotihuacan influences, we were also alert to the possibility of other Mexican impacts on the Maya, namely those of Toltec inspiration. In this regard, our findings turned out to be more exciting and important—or so we think—than those pertaining to Teotihuacan. Specifically, we feel that we discovered significant evidence that involves Toltec-derived cultures with the Classic Maya "collapse" of the ninth and early tenth centuries A.D. While any Maya archaeologist working in the southern lowlands can always claim to have been on the lookout for clues that will tell us more about the collapse, it should be stated that we did not choose Altar de Sacrificios with this particular problem in mind. It was incorporated into our research strategy as an afterthought, midway through the fieldwork period, when we had begun to control and appreciate our ceramic and pottery figurine data and see their implications.

In addition to these kinds of questions, initially historical but with functional and processual implications, we were also interested in the nature of settlement patterns in the Altar de Sacrificios region and in the implications that these held for sociopolitical and socioeconomic interpretations of ancient Maya society. I had recently concluded the Belize Valley settlement study (Willey et al. 1965) on the relationships of house-mound or small-structure distributions to ceremonial centers, so questions of this nature were still very much on my mind in 1958 (see also Bullard 1960; Willey and Bullard 1965).

THE EXCAVATIONS AND OPERATIONS

The field operations at Altar de Sacrificios were under the immediate direction of A. L. Smith. These were begun in early 1959, with the clearing of the site and the making of an instrument map, the latter being delegated to W. R. Bullard, Jr. (Willey and Smith 1969, fig. 4).

Large-scale excavations commenced the next season, in 1960. These were begun in Group B (fig. 2). The Group B structures are arranged around a small rectangular plaza. A pyramid 13 meters high, which is the tallest mound at the site, is on the south side of this plaza. This is Structure B-I. Structures B-II and B-III, on the west and north sides of this plaza, are smaller pyramids. The fourth structure, designated as B-IV, forms the east side of the group. Its total bulk is larger than that of any of the other B Group mounds, although it is not as high as Structure B-I, and its general form is best described as a complex palace-type platform mound with terraced upper platform and court arrangements. Smith began by clearing the north, or plaza, side of the pyramid, Structure B-I. He first exposed the red-sandstone-block and clay-mortar-masonry covering to this pyramid which had been its final architectural phase. Although sections of the masonry were still in position, other portions had been dislodged and jumbled by root action. In conjunction with this clearance of the north face of B-I, deep tests were also put down in the plaza floor immediately in front of the pyramid. These went to depths of over 3 meters before striking sterile soil. This plaza accumulation, while containing abundant potsherd refuse, was essentially fill that had been brought in during the building of the Group B structures. Subsequent deep exploratory cuts into the north face of B-I disclosed a series of superimposed building levels. While the red sandstone outer coating of the pyramid, to which we have referred, was shown to have been constructed in Protoclassic times, the two immediately underlying architectural levels dated from the Late Preclassic Period. Both had been surfaced with a masonry composed of lime-encrusted river shells or *almejas*. The next two underlying structural levels were coated, respectively, with a mixture of calcareous material and small stones, and with burned earth and gravel. These, too, were of Late Preclassic date. Underlying these were two still earlier levels, the sixth and seventh, respectively, from the top down. The sixth level, for which our excavation exposure was of very limited extent, presented a mound coating of thick plaster over a base of burned earth and gravel. Its date is either terminal Middle Preclassic or very early Late Preclassic. The seventh and earliest building was a low mound surfaced only in burned clay and dating to the Middle Preclassic Period. It was underlaid by a stratum of clay, sand, and refuse which contained Middle Preclassic sherds of the San Felix and Xe phases, the last named representing the earliest occupation of Altar de Sacrificios.

The smaller pyramids of B Group, Structures B-II and B-III were also excavated in depth, and they revealed a constructional history similar to that of Structure B-I. Their final coatings of Protoclassic (Salinas phase) date were of red sandstone, their intermediate ones of lime-encrusted shell masonry, and their earliest ones of ground stone and lime mortar. Deep but narrow tests in the B-IV complex gave a similar stratigraphy.

Burials and caches were found at various points in the Group B excavations. Of special interest was the discovery of a large cache (or series of caches) of pottery vessels immediately below the sandstone outer coating of B-I. These apparently composed a dedicatory cache placed there just prior to the completion of the final architectural phase of this pyramid. The vessels of the cache were of Protoclassic (Salinas phase) types. Another noteworthy feature was a Late Preclassic burial in Structure B-III, one end of which was enclosed in a crude corbeled vault of red sandstone blocks. This, however, was not a true vault since the stone blocks rested on clay fill rather than upon stone walls. No typically Maya vaulted structures, either standing or fallen, were encountered in any of our B Group digging.

A number of motivations, born out of general exploratory curiosity, guided the Group B excavations. To begin with, we were anxious to know how the pyramids and their ceramic contents would relate to the Early Cycle 9 stelae that were found on the north face of Structure B-I. We also wanted to know more about the strange red sandstone architecture, an anomaly for the Maya lowlands. Once work had begun, and the presence of Preclassic architectural levels in the B Group pyramids had been disclosed, we were then most interested to see what in the way of a civic-religious center could be attributed to the Preclassic Period and how far back in time such features might be identified. For, as of 1959-1960, there was very little known about Maya lowland Preclassic architecture. The Uaxactun explorations (Ricketson and Ricketson 1937; A. L. Smith 1950) had uncovered Temple E-VII-sub, of Late Preclassic or Protoclassic date, as well as some other Late Preclassic platforms; but this was only one site, and it still remained to be seen to just what degree Maya Preclassic cere-

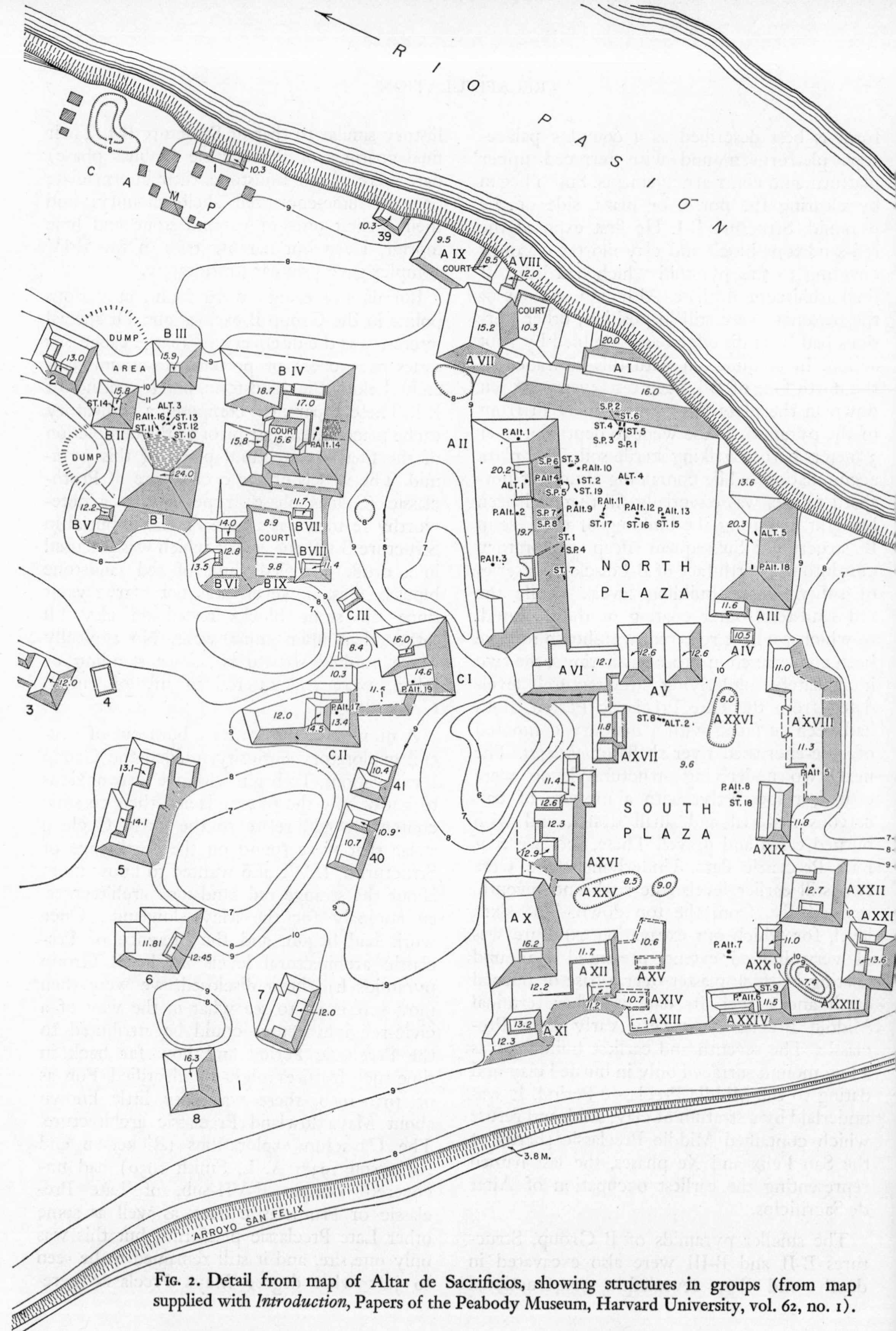

Fig. 2. Detail from map of Altar de Sacrificios, showing structures in groups (from map supplied with *Introduction*, Papers of the Peabody Museum, Harvard University, vol. 62, no. 1).

1–8 House mounds not assigned to groups
AI–CIII Structures in groups
• ALT. Altar
• P.Alt. Plain Altar
— ST. Stela
— S.P. Sculptured panels
Contour interval is 1.0 meter
Elevation on top of Altar 4 is 10.0 meters

monialism, and sociopolitical complexity, foreshadowed that of the Classic Period. The results of this line of inquiry were, we feel, rewarding, and our principal regret in connection with the Group B work is that we were unable to devote more time, money, and men to the clearing of larger exposures of the deeper Preclassic structures.

The excavations in Group B were continued through the 1961, 1962, and 1963 seasons; and during these seasons we were also at work in Group A. Group A is larger than Group B, lies immediately to the east of it at the east end of the site, and measures about 400 meters north–south and 200 meters east–west. It is divided into North and South Plazas of about equal size. The large mounds A-I, A-II, and A–III enclose three sides of the North Plaza. In extent and bulk they are the largest mounds at Altar de Sacrificios. Structure A-II, which is still largely intact, is over 100 meters long; however, neither it nor the others are quite as high as Structure B–I. All three of these big A Group structures are oblong platform mounds. All were built up of successive building layers of fill and masonry facings. The North Plaza is bordered on its remaining, or south, side by a smaller palace structure, A-VI, and by a ball court, A-V. A number of platform mounds, none as large as the big ones around the North Plaza, enclose and form the South Plaza. The arrangement here is not quite as precise as in the North Plaza, but there is the same general orientation to the cardinal points of the compass. There were no standing buildings on any of the mounds in either plaza of A Group at the time of our work at the site, nor had any been reported by earlier investigators.

In A Group, Structure A-I, a palace-type complex, was first cleared and cut down along its eroded riverbank face. After this, a deep cut was made on an east–west axis, bisecting the main body of this large platform and exposing its many complex structural features.

Additional tests were also made in the platform, and on its upper terraces a number of surmounting platform structures were wholly or partially cleared. All of these excavations enabled us to define three major building phases for Structure A-I. The two earliest were characterized by red sandstone terrace facings, and the last phase was of limestone blocks. Pottery in the various levels of the architectural fill indicated a terminal Early Classic to a Late Classic constructional history. Stelae 4 and 5, both of the seventh century A.D., had been incorporated in the outer structural covering and helped to establish the final Late Classic date.

Structure A-II, the very long platform mound on the west side of A Plaza, also proved to be entirely of Classic date. Its earliest building levels were of sandstone and its three later ones of limestone. Most of our digging was on the plaza, or east, side of this structure although some excavations were made in its summit. The associated stelae on the east side confirm a Late Classic dating for the limestone building levels.

Structure A-III, on the east side of A Plaza, was excavated on its west face and summit and also proved to be of Classic Period age. In addition, there was some evidence of Jimba phase, or Early Postclassic Period, building at one end of the structure. A notable feature of A-III was a deep crypt burial. The occupant (Burial 128) was a middle-aged female (40-44 years) who had apparently been interred with great pomp. She had been accompanied by numerous pottery vessels, jewelry, and paraphernalia; and it is possible that a younger female (25-29 years) (Burial 96) had been buried in a nearby grave at the same time and as an immolated sacrifice. The individual in the Burial 96 grave was accompanied with an unusually handsome polychrome cylinder jar of Pasión phase (Late Classic) date, and the painted scenes on this vessel may represent the joint funeral ceremony of the two individuals in question.[9]

A good many other burials were found in Structure A-III and also in Structure A-I; and

9. The reader is referred to Adams (1971, pp. 59–78) for a discussion and interpretation of these two burials and the pottery vase in question. See also Smith (1972, pp. 259 and 266–268) for descriptive itemizations of these burials and Saul (1972) for photographs (figs. 10, 11) as well as health and other biologic data obtained from these skeletons (tables 8,10,13,15,20, 22).

various caches of artifacts were found beneath some of the altars and stelae in A Group.

Other explorations in A Group included the excavation of Structure A-V, an open-ended ball court which probably dates from the Pasión phase of the Late Classic Period.

Throughout, the explorations in Group A were essentially those with descriptive and chronological goals. We were interested in finding out about continuity or discontinuity in the growth of the site. Dated stelae in Groups B and A indicated that the latter succeeded the former as the main ceremonial center of Altar de Sacrificios. When had this shift taken place? Did it correspond to the Initial Series or stelae hiatus that marks the end of the Early Classic Period elsewhere in the southern lowlands? And, more generally, how could all of the various aspects of Altar—architecture, arts, ceramics, and artifacts—be coordinated or synchronized in a site chronology?

Group C is not really a plaza arrangement but is the designation given to three structures, two of medium size and one quite small, which are situated to the southeast of Group B and to the southwest of the North Plaza of A Group. Large depressions surround Group C on all sides, and, while these are partly natural, they were undoubtedly enlarged by the "borrowing" of soil for the construction fills of the mounds of Group A, B, and C. Our operations in Group C were minor, being limited to a single deep test in Structure C-I, a medium-sized platform. We found the earlier levels of this building to be clearly Preclassic, with *almeja* masonry construction similar to that of Group B. The later levels of Structure C-I were more difficult to date. The building may have received Late Classic additions, but this has remained uncertain.

The smaller outlying mounds of Altar de Sacrificios, referred to as the house mounds, are located to the west of Groups A, B, and C. These house mounds are either simple rectangular platforms or rectangular platforms with one, two, or more terrace levels or subdivisions. Little facing stone was used in their construction. We counted a total of 41 such mounds, all but one of them located within a radius of 700 meters to the west of Group B. The single exception, Mound 38, was on a tiny patch of high ground more than a kilometer farther west than the others. Forty of these mounds were excavated. It was found that some of them had been domestic platforms since Preclassic times, and, indeed, it was in one of them that we first discovered Xe phase pottery, the earliest known from the site. We were concerned primarily with two things in these small structure excavations: to determine their function and to get some idea of the changes in the numbers of constructions or occupations through time. With regard to the first objective, we are fairly certain that these platforms, for the most part constructed of clay, were used as bases for buildings of wood, wattle, and thatch and that the primary function of these buildings was to provide places of domestic residence. The nature of the refuse, the location of the platforms, their relative size in comparison to the civic-ceremonial constructions, and their homologous and analogous relationships to other such features in Maya lowland sites support the assumption. As to the second question, our tests showed that there were relatively few such houses in the Middle Preclassic Period, that there were considerably more in the Late Preclassic, that their number shrank in the the Early Classic, that it increased again and was largest of all in the Late Classic, and, finally, that it diminished greatly in the Jimba phase or Early Postclassic Period.

Beyond the limits of Altar de Sacrificios proper, as we have defined the site on our map (see Willey and Smith 1969, fig. 4), our settlement surveys were more limited in scope and casual in nature than we would have liked. Time and resources were simply not available to make an extensive survey of the lower Pasión-Salinas confluence region beyond the few observations and notes that we did make. However, a number of comments are possible even on the basis of these. To begin with, it seems unlikely that the residents of the 40-odd domiciliary mounds described could have built and sustained the Altar de Sacrificios center. The size of the B and A Group mounds, together with the stelae and other monuments of the site, suggest a larger support population; and our limited surveys in the lower Pasión region tend to bear this out. For instance, there are a good many single mounds or small clusters of house mounds along the shores of the lower Pasión and the neighboring course of the Rio Salinas. We know of some directly across the Pasión from Altar de Sacrificios—in actual distance closer to the Altar ceremonial center than is our distant Mound 38. Others occur at various locations up the Pasión toward Sayaxche. Besides these river-edge mounds there are still others farther inland away from the immediate course of the stream. Nor are all of these mere house mound or small platform mound sites. Some, such as El Pabellon, La Amelia, and El Caribe, have small ceremonial centers, with larger mounds and carved stelae, as well as house mounds. These are located within 5 to 15 kilometers of Altar de Sacrificios. Thus, tentatively, we see the outlines of a larger regional settlement pattern emerging from the data. Altar de Sacrificios appears as the principal center; other but lesser ceremonial centers lie within a radius of 15 kilometers from it; and scattered about among all of these, with some concentrations near the ceremonial centers, as in the small mound group to the west of the Altar main plazas, are separate house mounds and little clusters of mounds.

Beyond this Altar de Sacrificios regional pattern we glimpse the outlines of others.[10] Seibal (Willey and Smith 1967; Smith and Willey 1969), a major center larger than Altar, is located up the Rio Pasión at a distance of 50 airline kilometers from Altar de Sacrificios. It, too, was probably the dominant political and religious center in its region, which may have included the rather sizable minor centers of Aguateca, Dos Pilas, and Tamarindito. Downstream on the Usumacinta, we do not come to major ceremonial centers until we reach Yaxchilan, 65 airline kilometers to the northwest of Altar de Sacrificios. This great site was undoubtedly another important regional center if, indeed, its influence was not multiregional. Clearly, little is known about these wider aspects and implications of settlement pattern in the Maya lowlands, and in making these few preliminary remarks here we do not wish to speak as if questions of politico-religious territoriality in the old Maya lowland domain were in any way settled. These are problems for future research, at least insofar as anything truly detailed and demonstrable may be brought forward. However, in a very general way, there is a scope and scale to matters of this kind that is worth speculating about, and these observations on the Altar de Sacrificios, Seibal, and Yaxchilan regional spheres should be taken in that light.

To return to the central ruins of Altar de Sacrificios, no summary description of the site, however brief, can omit mention of the numerous stelae and altars found there. Maler first reported upon these; Morley began the study of their hieroglyphics and dates; and John Graham continued this work during the 1959 and 1961 seasons of the recent Altar expedition. Graham counted a total of 19 stelae, of which 16 are carved and three plain.[11] Stone altars number 29, a figure which includes seven that are carved, 19 that are plain, and three basin-shaped altars that are designated as "Censer Altars." These total counts include some new monuments discovered by us during our excavations and site clearing.

10. The reader is referred to Willey and Smith (1969, pp. 33–35, fig. 6) for a discussion of these wider aspects of lower Pasión Valley settlement and an accompanying map.

11. What might be called the "official" Altar de Sacrificios stelae numbering series runs from 1 through 21; however, in actuality we know of only 19, not 21, stelae. Stela 6, a number assigned by Maler (1908), refers to a stone fragment on Structure A–I, which is probably not a stela. Another fragment was designated as Stela 14 by Morley (1937–38), but it is unlikely that it was a stela. Rather than to create confusion with reference to previous literature on the subject of the Altar de Sacrificios stelae, John A. Graham (1972a, pp. 24 and 57–58) has retained this official numbering series, with references to the fragments known as Stelae 6 and 14. Incidentally, Morley (1937–38, vol. 2, pp. 320–321) places the "Stela 14" on Structure B–IX, a small outlier of B Group; Graham (1972a, pp. 57–58) so lists its location; however, A. L. Smith, who was one of the party that discovered this monument, insists that this location is in error and that the stone was actually found on top of Structure B–II.

On our map of this site (Willey and Smith 1969, fig. 4) it is placed on B–II.

Graham reinterpreted the dates of several of the monuments, establishing, among other things, that the earliest Altar de Sacrificios Initial Series date is to be read as 9.1.0.0.0 (A.D. 455). The latest of the Initial Series dates is 9.17.0.0.0 (A.D. 771). (These and other dates are given in the 11.16.0.0.0 Correlation.) The earlier monuments at the site proved to be made of red sandstone; the later ones were of limestone. In general, the hieroglyphic texts from these several Altar de Sacrificios stelae and altars compose a substantial contribution to the Classic Maya hieroglyphic corpus (see Graham 1972a).

Other operations in connection with the Altar de Sacrificios research went ahead, concurrently with the digging, in both the field and elsewhere. A field laboratory was established where thousands of potsherds were classified and tabulated, thereby providing the basis for our ceramic chronology of the site (Adams 1971). Other artifacts were studied at the site laboratory or brought to the United States for further examination.[12]

12. Preliminary statements on the Altar excavations are found in Willey et al. 1960; Willey and Bullard 1961; A. L. Smith and Willey 1962; and Willey and A. L. Smith 1963. The reader is also referred to the five unpublished preliminary reports on Altar that are to be found in the Peabody Museum Library, Harvard University, authored, variously, by Willey, A. L. Smith, W. R. Bullard Jr., J. A. Graham, R. E. W. Adams, M. Hoffman, J. Wilson, T. Fiske, and J. Ladd, and dating 1959–1963, inclusive.

II

CULTURE–HISTORICAL INTEGRATION

THE DETERMINATION OF CULTURE PHASES

By culture-historical integration I mean a time-ordered presentation of the several phases of culture that are represented in the deposits and constructions of a site such as Altar de Sacrificios. The primary concern is historical description, but it is description in a series of functioning contexts. To do this we must first segment the record at Altar into a series of culture phases. How does one define and set the typological and chronological boundaries to these phases? To what degree is this an arbitrary procedure or to what degree are the phases inherent in the data? The answer is that both conditions obtain. This will be recognized as the same question that has occasioned considerable debate about archaeological typology. I will take the position here that phases (and types) are not imaginary but are based upon phenomena of the real world—on archaeological objects as these are seen in their contexts. The arbitrariness of definition lies in the criteria that are selected to build our phases (or types) around. And these criteria must be selected according to one's interests and the problems to be confronted.

If the problems are to be the general and multiple ones of historical description, and this has been our primary concern in the treatment of the Altar de Sacrificios data, then we must select phase criteria that will enable us to examine culture change through time as this change can be observed in a number of media: architecture, major arts, hieroglyphics, ceramics, burial practices, settlement, and other material aspects of culture.

Can we define phases that will serve in such an all-purpose way? Will the same phases serve to measure change in pottery development and in architecture? In the case of Altar de Sacrificios, and probably most of the Maya lowland centers, the answer is that we would probably have to mark off our time scales somewhat differently for almost every aspect of culture in order to obtain the most precise appreciation of the various culture changes that have transpired; however, it is also likely that there are some points in the sequence of past events at Altar in which significant and notable changes in several aspects of culture came about more or less concurrently. Indeed, if culture is a system and its subsystemic parts are interdependent in their changes through time, one would anticipate some such degree of coordinate change.

The problems of phasing in Maya archaeology were aired at the 1965 Guatemala City conference on ceramics.

> Coe and Culbert raised the question, during the conference, of the best method of establishing phases and delimiting them in time. They pointed out that it is customary to establish the dimensions of phases by means of the boundaries of ceramic complexes, with other archaeological categories related secondarily to already established "ceramic phases." For Tikal an attempt will be made to consider the interrelationships of as many aspects of culture as possible before phase boundaries and characteristics are established. With this approach, it may be possible to place phase boundaries at points at which several cultural categories showed simultaneous accelerated change. (Willey, Culbert, and Adams 1967, p. 305.)

Our Altar de Sacrificios phase sequence was determined primarily by Adams with his ceramic study. There are good and conventional archaeological reasons for this that have been stated many times before. Pottery, at least in sherd form, is abundant in Maya sites, and it is found in virtually all contexts in those sites. Thus, through its use one can establish contemporaneity, or lack of contemporaneity, between site features which can be dated in no other way. At the outset at Altar it was evident that ceramics could serve in this way and also provide us with more chronological subdivisions—thereby giving us a more finely-scaled appreciation of culture change through time—than Smith's architectural periodization, Graham's readings of the Maya Initial Series dates, Saul's physical anthropological data, or what I could offer from the nonceramic artifacts. But, in agreement with Coe and Culbert, I think it will be of interest to see how Adams' ten ceramic phases coordinate, or fail to coordinate, with other kinds of change. For in the study of the variability and covariability of culture change we will position ourselves to learn more about the processes involved. We have not taken the Coe-Culbert advice and attempted to refashion our Altar culture phases. Their suggestion came well after the close of the Altar fieldwork and most of the analyses; however, the exercise in a comparative examination of change in our sequence seems well worthwhile, even if offered only in a preliminary way.

To begin at the early end of the time scale, the change from our Xe phase to our San Felix phase is carried largely by ceramics. Part of our difficulty here is that we have few other data on these early time levels. There is, notably, a first appearance of artificial platform mounds in the San Felix phase. These had not occurred in Xe. However, these do not appear at the Xe-San Felix ceramic dividing line, but, insofar as we can be precise, toward the end of the latter phase.

With the succeeding Plancha ceramic complex come notable architectural changes, in mound size, masonry techniques, and special building features. In addition, there are settlement pattern changes, with a sudden increase in numbers of house mounds; and there are some artifactual innovations, such as the first appearance of jadeite. Now while there is some buildup of these things throughout the Plancha phase, there nevertheless is the impression that the San Felix-Plancha dividing line is a boundary of greater concurrent change than the previous phase boundary.

The next boundary, between Plancha and Salinas, might be described as more blurred or more drawn out than the San Felix-Plancha one. A number of ceramic innovations begin showing up in the latter part of the Plancha phase. These climax or culminate in Salinas, but they have been very clearly foreshadowed. On the other hand, a major shift in architectural materials—the appearance of red sandstone masonry—does not come about until the inception of Salinas.

The Salinas-Ayn boundary is marked by ceramic changes, with the first appearances of Classic Maya or Tzakol-like polychromes, and it is also marked by the first appearance of carved stelae and Initial Series dates and hieroglyphs. But at Altar, little or nothing transpires architecturally; in fact the temple precincts that continue in use are the same ones that were built in Salinas times.

The two relatively brief phases, Veremos and Chixoy, date from the period of the Classic Maya stelae hiatus—plus, perhaps, a decade or so later. These phases may be distinguished ceramically from what has gone before, from each other, and by what comes after. Red sandstone continues as the major architectural material, and at some point in the span covered by these two phases there was a shift in the main ceremonial plaza of the site from B Group to A Group. Our study of the Veremos and Chixoy phases is handicapped by relatively little archaeological material although this in itself may be a clue to significant change. Certainly, from what we know of other sites in the southern lowlands this brief epoch, from Early Classic to Late Classic in the Maya sequence, must have been a time of important concurrent change; and I am inclined to feel that at Altar de Sacrificios it was, even though we cannot document this in a very satisfactory manner.

Between the Chixoy and the Pasión phases there are some ceramic changes, but there is also a clear continuity of the Maya Late Classic pottery tradition. At Altar this is a major point of change in architecture. The A Group Plaza remains as the ceremonial center of the site, but limestone replaces red sandstone as the basic building material in the first oblong platform mounds at the site. The Chixoy-Pasión boundary, or a point in time very close to it, also marks the revival of the stelae cult. There are in addition a number of artifactual innovations, such as in the appearance of moldmade figurines and of numerous stemmed projectile points; and active trade with the seacoast is attested in such things as marine shells for ornaments and the presence of sting-ray spines in burials and caches.

The Pasión-Boca boundary is also marked by a number of concurrent changes. There is a partial severance of old ceramic traditions and an inauguration of new ones. This is correlated with a near-cessation of major architectural activity and stelae dedication. But in settlement it is correlated with what appears to have been a population increase, both for the Altar locality and for the lower Pasión Valley.

The Boca-Jimba boundary is defined by a complete ceramic tradition replacement which we have interpreted as a population replacement as well.

Looking back over this sequence, we see several points or phase boundaries that are impressive in that they mark a concatenation of change in various aspects of culture, and in this preliminary survey we have by no means exhausted all of the changes that define these boundary lines. All such boundaries of multiple change correlate with ceramic change and with the ceramic phases which Adams has defined; however, some of his ceramic-change boundaries are not marked by notable concurrent change in other aspects of culture. This is not intended as a criticism of Adams nor of our Altar de Sacrificios phase sequence. I think that he operated in the only way that he could, given the state of knowledge of Maya lowland archaeology as of the early 1960s. Adams was, to a great extent, guided by comparative correlations with what was known of sequences at other sites, particularly Uaxactun, and he tended to use similar criteria (ceramic) in making his phase definitions. At the same time, the points raised by Coe and Culbert at the 1965 conference are important ones. We should be more alert to the differentials of change in the various aspects of culture whether or not we attempt to formalize these by combining or incorporating them into our culture phase definitions.

CHRONOLOGY AND DATING

Before describing the content of our Altar de Sacrificios phases we should lay down some chronological definitions. By chronology I mean, in this context, both relative and absolute chronology; and, with reference to the latter, we shall be concerned with specific B.C.–A.D. dates.

The culture sequence or relative chronology at Altar de Sacrificios has been constructed largely through ceramic and architectural stratigraphy at that site. This has been abetted by cross-references to other Maya lowland archaeological sequences. The absolute chronology at Altar is keyed, primarily, to the Initial Series dates of the Maya calendar as these occur on the monuments at the site. Radiocarbon dates have given additional support to these Maya dates; and, again, cross-referencing to other Maya lowland sites, where stelae dates and radiocarbon dates are available, has been a further aid in this construction of an absolute chronology. The cross-references to which we refer are carried mainly by the matching of ceramic types and styles from one sequence to another.

We feel that the Altar relative chronology is secure, that there can be no question about the time order of the several culture phases. There is, however, room for argument about our absolute chronology or dating scale, and the questions concerning it need some review. This review follows.

Before going to the Altar data, however, let us review the more general framework of Mesoamerican archaeological chronology. It is now generally accepted that a Mesoamerican Early Preclassic (or Early Formative, if you prefer) Period begins somewhere around the date 2000 B.C. The radiocarbon dates on the Purron and Pox potteries of the Tehuacan Valley and the Guerrero coast are a few hundred years earlier than this (MacNeish, Peterson, and Flannery 1970); so if one defines the floor of the Early Preclassic on the appearance of ceramics, then the beginning date should be pushed back a bit. On the other hand, if full

11.16.0.0.0 CORRELATION	TIME	MAJOR PERIODS		ALTAR DE SACRIFICIOS		UAXACTUN	TIKAL		BARTON RAM
	1500	POSTCLASSIC							
11.10.0.0.0	1400								
	1300								
11.0.0.0.0	1200								
	1100								
10.10.0.0.0	1000			POST JIMBA			CABAN		NEW TOWN
	900			JIMBA					
		CLASSIC	Terminal	BOCA	Late Facet	TEPEU 3	EZNAB		SPANISH
10.0.0.0.0	800				Early Facet				LOOKOUT
	700		Late	PASIÓN	Late Facet	TEPEU 2	IMIX		
					Early Facet				
9.10.0.0.0	600			CHIXOY		TEPEU 1	IK		TIGER RUN
				VEREMOS		3		Late Facet	
	500			AYN	Late Facet				
					Early Facet				
9.0.0.0.0			Early			TZAKOL 2	MANIK	Early Facet	HERMITAG
	400								
	300			SALINAS		1			
8.10.0.0.0	200	PRECLASSIC	Proto-Classic				CAUAC-CIMI		FLORAL PA
	100				Late Facet		CAUAC		MOUNT HO
8.0.0.0.0	A.D. B.C.								
	100			PLANCHA		CHICANEL			
7.10.0.0.0	200		Late		Early Facet		CHUEN		BARTON CRE
	300								
7.0.0.0.0	400			SAN FELIX	Late Facet	MAMOM	Late Facet	TZEC	JENNEY CREEK La Fac
	500				Early Facet		Early Facet	EB	Ear Fac
6.10.0.0.0	600		Middle						
	700								
6.0.0.0.0	800			XE					
	900								
	1000								
	1500								

FIG. 3. A chronological diagram for Altar de Sacrificios and other Maya lowland sites. Dating follows 11.16.0.0.0 correlation and the generally accepted Major Period scheme of Mesoamerican archaeology. (This same chart has been reproduced in other Altar de Sacrificios monographs.)

agricultural sedentism is taken as the criterion of the inception of the Preclassic, then the date might be set at two or three centuries after 2000 B.C. Of course, the time of the establishment of the condition of "village farming" is also open to some debate (MacNeish 1967); early settled village life may have been based on other modes of subsistence (Coe and Flannery 1967; Green and Lowe 1967). But, accepting a beginning date of approximately 2000 B.C. for the Early Preclassic, it once had been customary to close that period and begin the Middle Preclassic at about 800 B.C. This latter date was the accepted approximate date of the first appearances of the Olmec style at La Venta (Drucker, Heizer, and Squier 1959), although some authors rounded this off slightly earlier, at 1000 B.C. (Willey 1966, figs. 3–8, 3–9). More recently, however, new radiocarbon dates from the Olmec site of San Lorenzo (M. D. Coe 1968) place the beginnings of the Olmec monumental style at about 1150 B.C., and arguments have been advanced (Berger, Graham, and Heizer 1967; Heizer 1968) for revising the La Venta dates downward in essential conformity with this. In accommodation to this, it has been suggested that the floor of the Middle Preclassic Period also be revised downward (Green and Lowe 1967, p. 55). I am in sympathy with this for if the Olmec style turns out to be a useful horizon marker—as there are indications that it might be from the early dates of its appearance in the Valley of Mexico (Tolstoy and Paradis 1971)—it could well serve as a period line in the same way that the Chavin horizon has so served in Peru (Rowe 1960). However, some archaeologists have, so far at least, retained the old period structure and refer to the Olmec style as having its inception in the latter part of the Early Preclassic Period. This difference in systematics is probably not of great moment, but, like some other terminological differences, it can be a source of confusion. To bring it home to our concerns with Altar de Sacrificios, it should be noted that the chronology chart which we show here as figure 3 and which was prepared by R. E. W. Adams in 1968, marks the beginning of the Middle Preclassic Period at 1000 B.C. This is the same chart that was first published in our "Introduction" (Willey and Smith 1969) and that has also been reproduced in *Artifacts* (Willey 1972) and *Human Skeletal Remains* (Saul 1972).

The terminal date for the Middle Preclassic Period has been placed variously, at from about 500 to 300 B.C. For the Maya lowlands this date has been based upon the inception of the Chicanel ceramic sphere (Willey, Culbert, and Adams 1967, fig. 10) which marks the beginning of the Late Preclassic Period. Radiocarbon dates for the Tikal Chuen Chicanel ceramic complex begin even a bit later than this, at 200 B.C. (Adams 1971, p. 147); however, the date of 300 B.C. has been taken as the Middle Preclassic-Late Preclassic dividing line on our figure 3 chart.

A Terminal Preclassic or Protoclassic Period has been dated variously in the Maya area and southern Mesoamerica. In terms of ceramic typology this is the horizon of the mammiform tetrapodal bowls and the first appearances of polychrome decoration in ceramics. Generally, the Protoclassic has been placed in the early centuries A.D. (e.g., Willey et al. 1965, fig. 3). In so placing it archaeologists have been aided by the fixing of the inception of the lowland Maya Early Classic Period by the first Initial Series stelae dates, which fall in the latter part of the third century A.D. It has been a convention to round this off at A.D. 300, as Adams has done in our figure 3.

The Early Classic Period has been tied to the Maya Initial Series dates of the latter part of Cycle 8 and the earlier part of Cycle 9. The close of the Early Classic is generally placed at A.D. 600, a round-figure compromise which approximates the end of the Classic Maya stelae hiatus at 9.8.0.0.0, or A.D. 593. This hiatus began just after 9.5.0.0.0., or A.D. 534, and it may be that a date at the beginning of the hiatus would be a better one for the Early Classic-Late Classic dividing line (see Willey, Culbert, and Adams 1967, fig. 10); however, our chart (fig. 3) uses the A.D. 600 convention.

The great Maya Classic florescence belongs to the seventh and eighth centuries A.D., with this chronology well-documented by numerous stelae dates from all parts of the southern lowlands. The ninth century A.D., the final century of the Late Classic, is the time of the Maya Classic decline in ceremonial-center construction and stelae carving. This is sometimes designated as the Terminal Late Classic (see fig. 3).

The Postclassic Period is usually then dated from A.D. 900 until the European incursions of the early sixteenth century.

The Altar de Sacrificios site sequence has been fitted into this general chronological framework of periods in the following fashion.

The Xe ceramic complex, which defines the Xe cultural phase, is the earliest at Altar de Sacrificios. Its typology has been compared to that of other southern Mesoamerican pottery complexes of the Chiapa de Corzo region, of the Chiapas and Guatemalan Pacific coasts, of the Guatemalan highlands, of the Peten, and of the southern Mexican Gulf coast. The closest parallels are with those which are conceded to fit to a middle Middle Preclassic time range, a horizon which is essentially post-Olmec style. Two Altar radiocarbon dates on the phase can be construed as generally consistent with this placement. One of them, (GX-172) the more securely associated, is from a definite Xe phase burial. Its one sigma span is 930–560 B.C. The other date (GX-163) was run on a sample of charred jack beans *(Canavalia ensiformis)* (see Willey 1972, p. 248). Our original field association of this sample was that of the subsequent San Felix phase; however, Adams (1971, p. 169) has suggested that the ceramic associations leave the bean specimens open to either a Xe or San Felix dating. The date of 1010–750 B.C. (with a one sigma span) is more easily accommodated to a Xe phase context. Adams (1971, table 26, pp. 146–151) would favor a starting date for Xe at Altar at about 750 B.C. I, too, would prefer this; and I think that his minimum range of 750–600 B.C. is probably about right. However, he gives a maximum range of 900–500 B.C. and settles for 900–600 B.C. on the figure 3 chart. This last has been our standardized or official projection for the Xe phase (for example, see the various tables in A. L. Smith 1972).

The San Felix phase, which follows the Xe at Altar de Sacrificios, features a ceramic complex that is a component member of the Mamom ceramic sphere (Willey, Culbert, and Adams 1967). As such, it is expectably on a late Middle Preclassic time level. Our radiocarbon dates—all from the earlier levels of the Group B architectural complex—give some support to this. GX-165, a charred maize sample, offered a date with a range of 620–380 B.C. which is right on the mark for the full San Felix-Plancha transition level from which the maize came. Two specimens from supposedly Xe-San Felix transition levels, GX-162 and GX-164, yielded dates of 409-81 B.C. and 420-170 B.C., respectively. Both are a little too late for what we would anticipate. Specimen GX-171, originally designated as "charred beans" but later identified as maize, gave a reading of 240 B.C.–A.D. 210, substantially later than expected. Adams, on his table 26 chart (Adams 1971, see pp. 146–151), makes a minimum dating estimate for San Felix of 500–350 B.C., a maximum of 600–200 B.C., and settles for 600–300 B.C. as our standardized estimate as given in figure 3.

There are no Plancha associated radiocarbon dates at Altar de Sacrificios, but as Plancha is a part of the Chicanel ceramic sphere various cross-datings are of assistance in helping us arrive at an estimate. There is little doubt but that the time position of the phase is the Late Preclassic Period: however, the close ties between some Plancha ceramics and those of the Cauac phase of Tikal, which is dated by radiocarbon at A.D. 0–150, leads us to extend the Plancha phase into the Protoclassic Period. Adams's (1971 table 26, pp. 146–151) maximum range for Plancha is 350 B.C. to A.D. 200, the minimum range 200 B.C. to A.D. 150, and his compromised standard dating (as given on fig. 3) 300 B.C. to A.D. 150.

In line with this terminal dating for Plancha, the following Salinas phase at Altar should begin at A.D. 150. This is somewhat late if we consider the ceramic typology of Salinas to be very similar to that of the Protoclassic Period and if that Period (fig. 3) has a dating of A.D. 0–300. However, Adams's principal reasons for making this dating arrangement are, again, linked to comparisons with Tikal. There, the Cauac phase, which shows strong late Plancha ceramic ties, had radiocarbon dates indicating an A.D. 0–150 time span; and the succeeding Cimi Cauac complex has some similarities to Salinas pottery. Our only Altar de Sacrificios radiocarbon date (GX–166) that might pertain to the Salinas is A.D. 105–415. In seeking a terminal date for Salinas we have some help from architectural stratigraphy and from a stela dedication date. The latest construction level of Structure B-I was built in late Salinas times. The earliest stela (Stela 10) associated with it bears the date of 9.1.0.0.0 (Graham 1972a, pp. 39–44) or A.D. 455. If we assume that this earliest stela was carved and dedicated shortly after the final building level of Structure B-I was completed, then the round date of A.D. 450 must be fairly close to the terminal date for the Salinas phase. This creates some trouble in cross-dating for it has generally been assumed that the Tzakol 1 subphase at Uaxactun (R. E. Smith 1955) begins at about A.D. 300 or maybe slightly earlier (see Willey, Culbert, and Adams 1967, fig. 10). At Altar de Sacrificios Tzakol 1-type pottery does not appear until the close of Salinas. This would suggest that A.D. 450 is too late for the close of Salinas. Adams (1971 pp. 146–151) has discussed this problem at considerable length, but he concludes by favoring the A.D. 450 date for the dividing line between Salinas and Ayn. The alternative is the more conventional cross-dating alignment which would place the Salinas-Ayn division at A.D. 300 (see Willey, Culbert, and Adams 1967). Following this line of reasoning, we would have to argue that Stela 10 was not erected until 150 years after the construction of Structure B-I. In my opinion, this stretches probability too far, and I would prefer to accept a time lag in the appearance of Tzakol-style pottery.

In line with our dating of Salinas, the Ayn phase is begun at A.D. 450 and is seen as largely contemporaneous with Uaxactun Tzakol 2. The early Ayn subphase or facet features the Z-angle bowl, the later the basal-flange bowl. The terminal date for Ayn is linked to the close of stelae dedication in B Group. The latest monument we have there (Stela 12) dates as 9.4.10.0.0. (A.D. 524); however, Graham (1972a, p. 116) is of the opinion that there may have been another monument in this series which we have not discovered and which was dedicated at 9.5.0.0.0 (A.D. 534). We think it almost certain that the Ayn phase lasted this long. This takes us up to the beginning of the hiatus in Maya Initial Series dates. Adams estimates the end of Ayn at 9.6.0.0.0 (A.D. 554), and this is followed on our chart (fig. 3); however, this is, admittedly, a "guess-estimate," within reasonable limits. Smith's guess is slightly later, at A.D. 570 (see A. L. Smith 1972, tables 3 and 5). With the data at hand, there is no point in attempting to mediate this small difference.

The dating of Veremos is largely guesswork, also, but again, within fairly restricted limits. The ceramic styles indicate a tailing off of the Tzakol tradition, and there are correspondences to Uaxactun Tzakol 3. However, I would estimate this to be the latter part of Tzakol 3 for there are no Teotihuacan influences in Veremos. These had occurred, instead, in late Ayn. The limited amount of evidence for Veremos phase activity at Altar, plus what cross-datings we can establish, would indicate a very short duration for the phase. Adams (1971, table 26) has set this at a single katun, from 9.6.0.0.0 to 9.7.0.0.0 or A.D. 554–573 while Smith makes the estimate of A.D. 570–585. In a broader frame of chronological reference, the Veremos phase is within the Initial Series hiatus, a point in Maya history at which we need fine-grained dating and detailed information. Unfortunately, we can do no better than this on our dating at Altar de Sacrificios.

The Chixoy phase also lacks radiocarbon dates,[13] and stelae dates give only approximate help in fixing its chronological limits. The ceramics of the phase show strong similarities to Tepeu 1 so there can be little doubt but that we are in the Late Classic Period. Architectural evidences for the phase at Altar are slight, and it is estimated that only a relatively brief span of time is involved. Adams (1971, table 26) sets the dates for Chixoy at A.D. 573 to 613, the closing date being the katun ending 9.9.0.0.0; Smith (1972, tables 3, 4, and 5), who begins Chixoy at A.D. 585, extends it to A.D.

13. There are two radiocarbon dates, GX–167, and GX–168, which come from mixed Chixoy-Pasión-Boca refuse contexts. The dates, however, are too early to be acceptable (see Adams 1971, table 2).

630. Three red sandstone stelae (Stelae 18, 8, and 9) may date to Chixoy, or they may belong to the beginning of the Pasión phase, depending upon whether the Adams or Smith estimates are followed. These three stelae are all from the South Plaza of A group, and they all were found near red sandstone buildings. Quite probably, they were originally associated with these buildings, and it is also highly likely that these buildings date from about the time of the dedications of the stelae which are, individually, 9.9.5.0.0 (A.D. 618), 9.9.15.0.0 (A.D. 628), and 9.10.0.0.0 (A.D. 633).[14]

The Pasión phase is the climax of the Late Classic Period at Altar. It is the time of the figure painted polychrome vessels that equate to Tepeu 2. Adams (1971, table 26) (see also our fig. 3) has dated Pasión from A.D. 613 to A.D. 771, or from 9.9.0.0.0. A number of stelae dates would fall within this range, including the three just mentioned. However, there are several later ones which are more definitely associated with Pasión architecture and ceramics, and the last of these (Stela 15) bears the date 9.16.18.5.1 (A.D. 769) and, presumably, was dedicated at 9.17.0.0.0 (A.D. 771). Adams's closing date for the Pasión phase is based on this katun ending. Smith (1972, tables 3, 4, 5) estimates Pasión as A.D. 630–780. John Graham (personal communication 1972) writes that he thinks A.D. 780 a better date than A.D. 771 for the close of the phase. In his words:

> The argument is that Stela 15, dedicated at 9.17.0.0.0. (A.D. 771), is a continuation of the previous stela erection pattern, is a "normal" stela, even a "prosperous" one, judging from the size. So the phase shift should be set a little later than 9.17.0.0.0, or say 9.17.10.0.0 (A.D. 780). It is after 9.17.0.0.0, not with it, that the stela erection pattern appears to be disrupted.

There are also three radiocarbon dates from Pasión: but only one of these (GX-170) at A.D. 560–790 is acceptable in terms of either the Adams or Smith estimates. The other two (GX-208 and GX-169) at 855–695 B.C. and 170 B.C.–A.D. 90, respectively, are too early to be acceptable.

The Boca phase at Altar de Sacrificios is clearly on the general Tepeu 3 time horizon, although it probably begins earlier than the Tepeu 3 subphase at Uaxactun or the Eznab phase at Tikal. These two phases, as well as the Bayal at Seibal, are thought to start at about 10.0.0.0.0 or A.D. 830 (Rands 1973), three katuns later than the Early Boca facet at Altar de Sacrificios. There is one monument at Altar (Stela 2), with a Giant Ahau date, which Graham (1972a, pp. 13–15) reads as 10.1.0.0.0 or A.D. 849[15] and which must have been dedicated during the Boca phase. There are also two possible Boca radiocarbon determinations (GX-167 and GX-168), but their dates are both (see Adams 1971, table 26) too early to help us in defining the chronology of the phase. Adams wants to end Boca at A.D. 909 or at katun 10.4.0.0.0, and Smith closes it at A.D. 900. This is approximately a katun later than the estimate for the close of Tepeu 3 at Uaxactun, but it is the same as for the end of the Tikal Eznab phase. Bayal, at Seibal, may or may not extend on slightly later. All of these phases, including Boca, show fine paste trade wares as horizon markers.

The Jimba phase at Altar, believed to represent the culture of an intrusive people, and characterized by an essentially pure fine paste ceramic complex, is dated as post-A.D. 909. Adams (1971, table 26) sets its terminal date at 9.6.0.0.0 or A.D. 948; Smith (1972, tables 3, 4, 5) has rounded this off to A.D. 950. As such, the phase falls in the Early Postclassic Period.

For convenience, the Adams and Smith datings are summarized. As stated previously, our figure 3 follows the Adams dates.

14. In this question of the Chixoy-Pasión division, the reader should consult Adams (1971, pp. 148–149) on architectural, ceramic, and stelae associations. Some errors in Adams's statements should be noted, however, although they do not greatly effect his line of argument. On his page 149, left-hand column, 8th line from top, the date in parentheses should read 642 A.D. rather than 633. In the same column, lines 16–18 down from top, the discussion of the latest sandstone monument should give the date of 9.10.0.0.0 (A.D. 633) for Stela 9. The date given, of 9.9.15.0.0. (A.D. 628) pertains to Stela 8. For further details on these and other Altar de Sacrificios monuments consult Graham (1972a).

15. Stela 2 was originally given the tentative date of 9.14.10.0.0 (A.D. 721) by Morley, and is so recorded in Smith's (1972) table 2: however, Graham's reading is much more probable.

	Adams Version	Smith Version
Xe phase	900–600 B.C.	Same
San Felix phase	600–300 B.C.	Same
Plancha phase	300 B.C.–A.D. 150	Same
Salinas phase	A.D. 150–450	Same
Ayn phase	A.D. 450–554	A.D. 450–570
Veremos phase	A.D. 554-573	A.D. 570–585
Chixoy phase	A.D. 573–613	A.D. 585–630
Pasión phase	A.D. 613–771	A.D. 630–780
Boca phase	A.D. 771–909	A.D. 780–900
Jimba phase	A.D. 909–948	A.D. 900–950

PRACTICAL DIFFICULTIES IN PHASE ASSIGNMENTS

A few last things remain to be said before beginning with our culture phase descriptions. These are concerned with the practical difficulties of making phase assignments. These difficulties involve all features, monuments, and artifacts at the site. Smith (1972) has discussed the phase placement of architectural features, burials, and caches, and, to some extent, that of the major monuments. Graham's (1972a) specific dating of the monuments is also related to phase assignments. Adams (1971) has been at pains to describe ceramic stratigraphy and the ceramic refuse content of building fills. In my study of the artifacts (Willey 1972) I have made phase assignments whenever possible and have usually explained, briefly, the basis of the assignment. As a study of all four of these monographs will show, there are many instances when such phase dating of features, monuments, pottery, or artifacts must remain only approximate. The Altar de Sacrificios site is physically complex, especially in its Groups A and B structures. These were almost all built in stages, many of them spanning the duration of more than one culture phase of the site's history. They incorporate fill material gathered from all parts of the site. Much of this fill contained midden refuse, including broken pottery and discarded artifacts; and, naturally, such detritus was constantly rearranged, collected, and redeposited out of its true chronological order as structures were being partially torn down, rebuilt, and added to. Frequently, the only stratigraphic or associational principle that could be applied was that refuse in fill was simply older than (or approximately contemporaneous with) the time of the construction of the building. And often even this basic archaeological rule was difficult to apply because of numerous intrusions through the mound structures—pits dug from upper floor levels down through earlier ones. Sometimes these pits had been made for burials or caches, and frequently they could be spotted and traced; but often they were difficult to see, were small, and of uncertain purpose. Such intrusions, naturally, brought later refuse materials into earlier contexts and made the job of sorting out the artifacts and features of Altar de Sacrificios by chronological phase more difficult.

A mention of these difficulties is not to say that they were insuperable; and, obviously, we think we had a certain success in overcoming them, at least for the most part. Otherwise any phasing or periodization of the remains would have been impossible. At the same time, we set down these words as a caution. In general, house mound or small structure stratigraphy is reliable, and pottery and artifacts found in superimposed levels in these minor buildings are most probably in proper chronological order. Ceremonial center structural stratigraphy is more open to complexities and error; but valid chronological order obtains here too, depending on the circumstances. Burials or caches are, of course, the prize associational units. Fortunately, we have a number of these although we could have done with more. But unfortunately, a great many caches from one particular provenience area, the north face of Structure B-I in its final constructional level, had been disturbed by tree root action and the slide and fall of stones and earth over the years. For these, we could recover the artifacts but in most cases not the original groupings; nor could we determine for certain if the original caches had been inclusive with, or intrusive into, the final construction phase of the pyramid.

One of our most difficult chronological or phase separations involves the last two Altar phases Boca and Jimba. There is no good vertical stratigraphy on the relationship of these two phases. The remains of both are found superficially over the site, especially the ceremonial center. There are, however, some horizontal separations of the two ceramic complexes which provide a basis for the definitions of each, and there are extra-site relationships for each that leave little doubt that the Jimba is the later of the two. It is, though, hard to be sure of the proper phase assignment in the case of many nonceramic artifacts which are found in what are best referred to as Boca-Jimba contexts (see Willey 1972).

Two other problems should also be noted. One of these has to do with functional interpretations, especially as these pertain to and derive from architectural features. The mixing of living refuse in building fills, especially in the larger structures, is apt to create confusion in this regard. Occasionally it could be determined that, for instance, a mano stone was very probably an original, functionally related artifact on a room floor; but more often such an interpretation could not be made with any degree of certainty. We could not be sure that we were not dealing with artifact detritus incidental to fill. And, deriving from this, we could not say with any assurance that such and such a building or room had been used for domestic purposes or not. Specifically, a great many "kitchen utility" objects, usually fragmented but sometimes not, were found during the excavations of the Group A palace-type buildings. We are inclined to think that there were living quarters on or immediately associated with these platforms, but there is an element of doubt in this interpretation.

The other problem is probably one of sampling. In itemizing the various artifacts that occur in our sequent phases at Altar de Sacrificios, I was struck by the fact that some types would make an appearance, then disappear for a phase or two, only to reappear again in a later phase. Assuming that the later reappearance was not a matter of an accidental inclusion of earlier fill material of the kind we have been describing, the question could be asked whether or not this appearance, disappearance, and reappearance reflected the true history of the type in question at Altar de Sacrificios.

Most probably, it did not. It was simply an effect of sampling or, more properly, inadequate sampling on our part. The appearance-disappearance-reappearance sequence is, of course, highly suspicious and easy to spot and to question. More difficult to interpret are those lacks of appearance of, say, marine shells in our earlier Altar de Sacrificios phases. Does their first appearance in the Classic Period phases reflect the true historical situation? Or have we just not exposed enough of the earlier occupation levels? As is to be expected, our sampling of the later phases—such as Pasión and Boca—is better than that of some of the earlier phases. These were the most readily available structures and refuse strata; these had to be cut through before we could go on to the more deeply buried earlier deposits. This matter of sampling is to be borne in mind as one reads through the successive phase descriptions, and I will call it to the reader's attention from time to time.

XE PHASE

The earliest occupation at Altar de Sacrificios, that of the Xe phase, is represented by pottery found over a wide area of the site. It occurs on the old ground surface under Group B Plaza, Structure B-I, and as far east as a point a little to the east of Structure B-IV. It was also found as the basal pottery in a number of the small mounds, or house mounds, to the west of B Group (as in Mounds 6, 24, 25, and 38). Besides these deposits, which are ranked as "occupations," occasional Xe sherds were found in eleven other house mounds (Smith 1972, table 3). In all instances the Xe sherds came from directly upon the old ground surface. This suggests that bush huts, of pole and wattle-and-daub walls and thatched roofs, were built directly on the surface at these locations. Some postholes were revealed under Mound 25, and wattle-daub fragments were found here as well as in some of the other Xe locations. Floors were the natural packed earth; and the location sites were probably selected as the slightly higher spots of the natural terrain. The most clearly defined of these natural packed earth floor surfaces was beneath the B Group Structures. It remains a moot point, however, as to whether or not the B Group area was a special or ceremonial center in Xe times. We found no evidences of platform building of any kind; and as far as the matter of concentration of refuse is concerned, more Xe sherd debris was found under Mounds 25 and 38 than below B Group.

A single burial (Burial 135) is identified with Xe phase. It was found in test-pit digging a short distance east of Structure B-IV, and it was from this burial that the osseous material of radiocarbon Specimen GX-172 gave the date of 930–560 B.C. (mean date: 745 B.C.). The individual was a young adult male (20–24 years), lying in a flexed position on his left side, head to northeast. There were no associated grave goods and no indications of any special tomb preparation. A simple pit had been dug into natural ground surface to receive the body. Quite probably, the burial had been made beneath a dwelling floor. The height of the individual is estimated at about 164 cm. His skull was undeformed with a cranial index of 82.2 (brachycranic or round-headed). The bones show no serious pathology although a well-healed fracture of the clavicle, slight lesions on the tibial tuberosities, and a possible premortem dent in the lamboidal area of the skull suggest the kind of stress injuries associated with athletics or strenuous activities in young persons. There were some dental caries and some premortem tooth loss as well as slight spongy or porotic hyperostosis.

Xe ceramics are, in great part, unslipped (Achiotes Unslipped: Raudal Variety) or monochromes (Abelino Red, Crisanto Black, and Huetche White). There is some two-color decoration (Toribio Red on Cream or Datile Red on Black) and some incision (Chompipi Incised, Pico de Oro Incised) and punctation (Baldizon Punctated). The Xe vessels tend to be thin-walled and may have been tempered with either sand or volcanic ash. The most typical forms are low-walled flat plates with everted rims, tecomates, and medium- and low-necked jars with handles. As such, this Xe pottery was fully adequate to serve as eating and cooking ware. Very large storage jars are missing although some of the tecomates would have had substantial volume, either for liquids or grains and seeds. The plate forms, especially, are pleasing to the eye, and the monochrome slipped surfaces, in red, black, or white, must have had a soft luster when such dishes were relatively new. The occasional bichrome painting and the incision and punctation were additional esthetic embellishments.

The Xe population also made pottery figurines, as well as vessels. These were small, solid, hand-made effiigies of humans, probably mostly females. Our sample is extremely limited and the pieces fragmentary; however, it is assumed that the style of the Xe figurines is much like that of the succeeding San Felix phase.

Perforated potsherd disks may date to the Xe phase and have been employed as spindle whorls. Two other ceramic items are probably associated with Xe. One is a hollow, perforated sphere, perhaps a rattle; the other is a modelled human face—too large for a figurine—which appears to be a fragment of a "mushroom-stand." It has been suggested (Borhegyi 1963) that such mushroom-stand objects had a cult significance in southern Mesoamerica in connection with the ritual use of hallucinogenic mushrooms. Other pottery mushroom-stands also occur in later Preclassic contexts (Plancha phase) at Altar (Adams 1971, figs. 19, 20). This putative Xe example came from beneath Structure B-II, and was in a stratum of Xe, plus some later Preclassic pottery. Its location in the B Group area might be taken as a possible bit of evidence for Xe phase ceremonial or ritual activities.

Another item that is a possible ceremonial feature, and that was found in B Group, is a little red sandstone table (as the type has been designated in the *Artifacts* monograph).[16] These red sandstone tables are small, four-legged, benchlike affairs, carved from single pieces of the soft, relatively lightweight Altar de Sacrificios sandstone. The function of such objects is not altogether clear; however, they seem rather friable and a utility purpose as an actual seat or small bench is doubtful. Hence, they may have had some ritual significance. The specimen in question was found in a Xe-San Felix mixed provenience in B Group, and it should be noted that nine other red sandstone tables were found in pure San Felix contexts in B Group. It may be that such "tables" are wholly confined to the later phase.

With the exception of a few miscellaneous worked stones, that may or may not have been tools, all Xe phase ground stone items are utility forms. The Xe metate was the ubiquitous basin-shaped or turtleback form, made of either limestone or conglomerate. All Xe manos were of the plano-convex variety. A rectangular type mortar can be associated to the phase, as can various celtiform and miscellaneous grooved and perforated stones. One polished stone celt (medium-sized) was also found in Xe debris. Many of these ground stone artifacts were taken from house mounds, but a substantial number also came from *in situ* midden debris under B Group, suggesting that if the later location did serve as a ceremonial precinct in Xe times it also served as a living site.

Chipped flint and chipped obsidian of the Xe phase is all within the utilitarian category, and such items came from both house mound locations and from under Group B. In flint, they include the general utility form of the chopper or celt, possibly some unifacial scrapers, and use-nicked and non-nicked flakes. In obsidian the only Xe items were the prismatic bladelets and some miscellaneous flakes. Of all the Xe industrial materials at Altar de Sacrificios only the obsidian need have come from a long distance, apparently from the Guatemalan highlands.

Except for some local freshwater mussel-shells, there were no shell materials in Xe phase deposits. Some pierced animal teeth were the only bone artifacts; however, deer bone scrap did occur in Xe middens.

A deposit of jack beans, in charred condition, was found in Structure B-III. These beans, identified as *Canavalia ensiformis*, date as either Xe or San Felix; but with the probabilities (see p. 18) favoring Xe. The radiocarbon date of 1010–750 B.C. (GX-163) was obtained from a sample of these beans.

The Xe community of Altar de Sacrificios, as we reconstruct it from the archaeological evidence, was, then, a small nucleation of forest and riverine farmers, probably not numbering over a hundred persons. Quite probably, other related communities may have been established along the lower Pasión at about the same time although we have no definite information about this. Almost certainly these early Xe settlers grew maize and prepared the land for this by clearing it with chipped stone celts. They must also have depended upon game and fish for some share of their subsistence although we have little data on the gear used in these pursuits. They built pole and thatch huts. There is little in their architectural remains or settlement evidences that would indicate that these early Altarians maintained anything other than an egalitarian community; however, the few odd ritual-type finds in probable Xe contexts in B Group hint at a politico-religious nucleus at this part of the site. Xe phase pottery is mostly monochrome ware and is represented in only a few vessel forms. Pottery figurines are handmade, solid, female effigies. There is little in any of these ceramic crafts that suggests luxury or high ritual pieces. We do not know for certain if this pottery and these figurines were made at, or in the immediate vicinity of, Altar de Sacrificios; but it is likely that they were. There is certainly nothing in the complex that could be designated as definite "trade pieces."

These observations on the relative simplicity of life of the Xe phase peoples at Altar de Sacrificios and of their seeming isolation from

16. Here, and elsewhere, further reference to artifacts is to be found in Willey (1972).

trade contacts with other pottery-making groups are not meant, however, to give the impression of a general cultural isolation. We have noted the presence of obsidian at Altar, and this indicates at least some extra-regional trade or contacts. Moreover, the Xe pottery and figurines are stylistically within a common, widespread, southern Mesoamerican Middle Preclassic tradition so that communications, however indirect had once existed, or continued to exist, with other regions. To begin close to home, in the Peten lowlands, Xe pottery can be assigned to the same ceramic sphere as that of another Xe complex found at Seibal, 50 kilometers to the east on the Pasión River (Smith and Willey 1969; Willey 1970).[17]

There are also relationships between Xe ceramics and those of the Mamom sphere complexes of Uaxactun (R. E. Smith 1955), Barton Ramie (Willey et al. 1965), and Tikal (Culbert, personal communication 1965). These Mamom sphere complexes are slightly later than Xe, of course, and are related still more closely to the succeeding San Felix complex at Altar de Sacrificios. There are also some resemblances between Xe ceramics and some of the early complexes of the northern lowlands, in Yucatan (Brainerd 1958, Andrews 1971, Joesink-Mandeville 1971); however, there are a number of striking differences, too, and it may be that these Middle Preclassic ceramics of the north have somewhat different origins than those of Xe and Mamom. Outside of the Maya lowlands, there are close resemblances between Xe and Chiapas-Guatemalan and Salvadoran highland pottery complexes. Dili and Escalera of Chiapa de Corzo (Dixon 1959, Warren 1961) are the best known of these; but the Frailesca (Navarrete 1960), Santa Cruz (Sanders 1961), and Mirador (Peterson 1963) should also be mentioned, as should the Pacific coastal Conchas 1 complex (M. D. Coe 1961). To these can be added the Kal complex of Chalchuapa in Salvador (Sharer and Gifford 1970). More recently, pottery discovered at Sakajut in the Alta Verapaz and at El Porton in the Baja Verapaz has been described as similar to Xe (Sedat and Sharer 1972; Sedat 1972; Sharer and Sedat 1972). As these regions are at the headwaters of the Chixoy-Salinas and Pasión drainages, I think that there is a probability of a close relationship between the Sakajut and El Porton ceramic complexes and Xe. Since Sakajut and El Porton pottery can be traced back to earlier Early Preclassic beginnings in the highlands, whereas it is the earliest pottery at Altar de Sacrificios and Seibal, there is a strong argument for deriving the Xe wares from the northern Guatemalan highlands and for seeing its makers as immigrants into the Peten from the highlands during the Middle Preclassic Period.

These Sakajut and El Porton similarities to Xe take on even more culture-historical significance in view of two other considerations. First, these upland sites are situated on trail systems which connect with the generally northward flowing rivers that descend into the Peten. Obsidian, jadeite, and quetzal feathers, all highland products and highly prized in the Peten, were undoubtedly traded over these land and water routes. As already noted, some of this trade, as evidenced by the obsidian, had begun as early as Xe times. Second, as we have emphasized, there is little in the Xe phase as seen at Altar that suggests the hierarchic elements of Maya culture; and this is generally true of other southern Maya lowland Middle Preclassic Period phases. But at Sakajut and at El Porton there are ceremonial platforms that are probably of Middle Preclassic date; and at El Porton there is a carved stela with hieroglyphs which dates from either Middle or Late Preclassic. The glyphs on this El Porton monument are in the Kaminaljuyu Late Preclassic tradition (Miles 1965), and, as such, are certainly possible prototypes for Maya Classic Period writing developments in the lowlands. In the light of these considerations, I think we must view the Alta Verapaz and the Baja Verapaz as potentially crucial regions in the development of Maya lowland Late Preclassic and Classic civilization.

These arguments, supporting an Alta Verapaz–Baja Verepaz-to-the-lowlands line of diffusion for early lowland populations and for later elements of high culture, differ from those expressed by Adams (1971, pp. 153–154) who, in his own work, had found little in these

17. Consult Willey (1970) for comparative considerations of the Xe ceramic complex.

highland regions to demonstrate such an origin and had, therefore, leaned toward Mexican Gulf coastal beginnings for Xe pottery. The Sakajut and El Porton findings were made since Adams expressed this opinion; but even more recently Adams (personal communication 1972) still expresses some doubts. He notes that the Polochic River Valley, which leads to the Izabal region and not to the Peten proper, is the easiest access route between the Alta Verapaz zone from the lowlands, and he offers the counterhypothesis that El Porton and Sakajut may represent a lowland-to-highland colonization rather than the reverse. In his words:

> . . . Xe is still an enigma as to origin and it may be a regionalized Peten culture already developed away from an earlier lowland ancestor culture which may be found farther out on the peripheries of the central lowlands–that is to say in the Polochic or Pusilha zones, or the Jatate, lower Usumacinta zones.

While admitting that present data are equivocal enough to allow the formulation of this hypothesis for Xe origins as an alternative, the lack of earlier Middle Preclassic complexes–at least from research so far in these peripheral zones–leads me to favor the highland-to-Pasión Valley interpretation at the present time.

Following out of the previous paragraphs, which have moved away from the Altar site itself, let us take an even wider view of the developmental trends of the Mesoamerican Preclassic, thus concluding this section on the culture-historical integration of the Xe phase at Altar de Sacrificios.

We know that at the close of the Early Preclassic Period (ca. 1200 B.C.), just prior to the Olmec horizon, there were settled, pottery-making village communities in a number of regions of southern Mesoamerica. The origins of some of these appear to go back as early as 2000 B.C. or even before (MacNeish 1967). All undoubtedly practiced some farming, but subsistence economies may have been mixed and regionally variable (M. D. Coe and Flannery 1967, Green and Lowe 1967). These Early Preclassic phases included the Ocos (M. D. Coe 1961) and Barra (Green and Lowe 1967) of the Guatemalan and Chiapas Pacific coasts, the Santa Marta Côtôrra of the Grijalva Basin of Chiapas (MacNeish and Peterson 1962), the pre-San Lorenzo components at that site in southern Veracruz (M. D. Coe 1968), Purron and Early Ajalpan in the Tehuacan Valley of Puebla (MacNeish, Peterson, and Flannery 1970), and the Pavon phase of the Huasteca coast (MacNeish 1954). At this early time there was little indication of what might be called elite class activity in any of these cultures except those of the pre-San Lorenzo phases. Of these, M. D. Coe (1968, pp. 45–46) has said:

> What is really remarkable, however, about these ancient horizons is the extraordinary amount of construction which must go back well beyond 1200 B.C. . . . The amount of work which must have been involved staggers the mind, for there are many thousands of tons of pre-San Lorenzo fill (consisting of earth, sand, clay, and bentonitic rock) which was brought in in basketloads to form Group D ridge alone. Furthermore, in Group D we came upon a deeply buried, and possibly temporary, stepped platform of sand and clay which is also pre-San Lorenzo.

For whatever reasons, these Early Preclassic Gulf coast cultures give signs of being more sophisticated than any of their Mesoamerican contemporaries. They had begun moving toward the development of ceremonial and politico-religious centers and toward a non-egalitarian society before any of the others.

A few centuries later, however, in what can be considered the early part of the Middle Preclassic Period (ca. 1200–900 B.C.) ceremonial centering, and its socio-political implications, are more widely seen in Mesoamerica. The extent to which these concepts were diffused from or stimulated by the Olmec centers are moot questions (see M. D. Coe 1968 and Flannery 1968). In any event, elite culture is represented at this time by the great coastal Olmec sites, with their mounds, monumental sculpture, and high art; and such things were beginning, if on a more modest scale, in the San Jose phase of Oaxaca (Flannery 1968) and in the Iglesia phase of the Valley of Mexico (Tolstoy and Paradis 1971).

By the middle and latter part of the Middle Preclassic Period, or from about 900 to 300 B.C., what we may call the ceremonial-centered society has become the general rule for southern and much of central Mesoamerica.

This would refer to the later Olmecoid phases of La Venta (Drucker, Heizer, Squier 1959; M. D. Coe 1968) and Tres Zapotes (Drucker 1943a), to the beginnings of the Ticoman culture in the Valley of Mexico (Tolstoy and Paradis 1971), to Late Ajalpan and Early Santa Maria of the Tehuacan Valley (MacNeish, Peterson, and Flannery 1970),[18] to Guadalupe and Monte Alban I in Oaxaca, to Arevalo and Las Charcas in the Guatemala Basin, to some of the early cultures of northern Yucatan to which we have already referred, and to many others. At this time only the Maya of the southern lowlands still appear to be on a simpler level of socio-political organization. However, even here too, as we shall see in our consideration of the San Felix Mamom phase at Altar, certain architectural signs point toward the beginnings of social differentiation.

SAN FELIX PHASE

The area of the San Felix settlement at Altar de Sacrificios was about the same as that of the Xe phase. A few more small mounds or house mounds showed San Felix pottery than had shown Xe ceramics. We recorded five definite occupations in the western part of the site, one probable occupation, and 14 instances of the presence of some San Felix sherds. For the first time these occupations were marked by definite artificial clay mounds. The dwellings had been built on these little platforms rather than on the natural ground surface as had been the case in Xe times. These little house platforms showed indications of what had probably been cooking fires; animal bone debris was found around some of them; and some had been used as places of burial.

The more important settlement and architectural changes between Xe and San Felix, however, are in the construction in B Group. Constructions G of Structure B-I, F of Structure B-II, F and E of Structure B-III, and an interior building of Structure B-IV all date from the late San Felix phase. The Structure B-I and Structure B-II platforms were of very modest proportions; but Construction E of Structure B-III had a height of 1.65 m, and the interior platform in Structure B-IV was at least 5 m high. These platforms were terraced and faced with lime-encrusted river shells, or *almejas*, laid up in mud mortar or, sometimes, in a kind of plaster made of ground-up *almejas*. Sometimes dressed red sandstone blocks had been used as stair steps or at the sides of stairs. Postholes were detected on the Construction E (of B-III) platforms, indicating former wooden posts. Judging from the size and features of these B Group buildings, it seems safe to state that by San Felix times there was a special ceremonial or civic plaza at Altar de Sacrificios. This ceremonial center, modest as it is, is the earliest one for which we have definite knowledge in the Maya southern lowlands, and it appears late in the Middle Preclassic Period.

Nine burials are identified with the San Felix occupation of Altar; seven of these date as straight San Felix and two as San Felix-Plancha.[19] All were simple pit interments, either flexed or extended on the back. One came from Mound 7, two from Mound 2, and the rest from B Group. All had been accompanied by at least one pottery vessel, and one multiple infant burial (Burial 127, #'s 1, 2, 3) had two pots. Other grave goods were rare.

18. See the general chronology chart (fig. 153) in MacNeish, Peterson, and Flannery (1970) for Mesoamerican-wide correlations.

19. See A. L. Smith (1972, table 5) for associational details on locations, grave goods, age, sex, head deformation, tooth filing or inlaying, and bone pathology. Smith (1972, tables 6–8) has additional detail on tooth filing and inlaying. See also Smith's Appendix B (1972, pp. 243–269) for a detailed description of all burials and their contents. See Saul (1972): table 8 for individual pathology, table 10 for individual sex and age evaluations, tables 12, 13 for individual stature estimates, tables 14, 15 for individual stature in conjunction with inferred social status and health status, tables 19–22 for individual dimensions and indices, and photographs of various individuals and their fragmentary remains.

One middle-aged (50–54 years) male (Burial 131) had a tiny greenstone bird-effigy pendant near the skull; and a young adult (25–29 years) male (Burial 129) was accompanied by a polished stone celt. Lambdoidal cranial flattening was noted on an elderly male of the San Felix-Plancha transition; however, this was not sufficient flattening to indicate true artificial deformation. The other San Felix-Plancha transitional burial, an adult and probably a female, had filed upper central incisors.

Bone and dental pathology was noted on several of these burials.[20] Burial 129, the young adult male (25–29 years), showed pronounced cranial osteitis, with lesions very much like those that would have been left by syphilis or yaws. In addition, the same man showed some signs of subperiosteal tibial hemorrhaging that together with his periodontal degeneration is suggestive of Vitamin C deficiency. Teeth showed abscesses, caries, and enamel hypoplasia. The latter condition, also noted on other San Felix and other Altar de Sacrificios burials of all phases, except Xe, where its presence or absence is uncertain, results from childhood malnutrition or disease. Another pathologic condition, probably reflecting childhood nutritional problems and, most likely, iron deficiency anemia brought on by chronic diarrhea, blood loss, and related problems, is spongy-porotic hyperostosis. This was seen on an elderly male (Burial 13) as well as on the cranium of a child (Burial 127 #1).

Of further physical anthropological interest is the height of the young male, Burial 129. This individual measured 170.75 cm (by conservative formula estimates). He was the tallest individual we found at Altar. Saul, in commenting on the Altar burials as a whole, observes a trend for Preclassic males to be taller than Classic Period ones and, also, for all pre-Columbian lowland Maya—at Altar de Sacrificios and elsewhere—to be generally taller than modern Maya. The pre-Columbian female Altarians were also taller than modern Maya women; however, within the Altar series no stature trend could be discerned for the females (Saul 1972, tables 3, 12–16, and chapter 2).

San Felix ceramics are identified as a part of the Mamom ceramic sphere. The most abundantly represented type is the unslipped utility ware, Achiotes Unslipped: Achiotes Variety. They also feature monochromes, which usually show a higher polish than do those of the Xe phase. There is a particularly heavy emphasis on the red (Joventud Red), but black (Chunhinta Black) and cream (Pital Cream) are also represented. There are positive-painted dichromes (Muxanal Red on Cream) and a resist red on gray. Plastic decorative techniques include champfering, grooved-incision, and zoned punctation. A Mamom sphere marker-type, the fine paste or temperless Mars Orange, is present but rare in San Felix. The most common vessel forms are necked jars (most often unslipped) and low-walled, flat-bottomed plates (monochromes). There are also composite-silhouette jars and bowls, some with everted rims. As in Xe, there is little in the ceramics that indicates special or luxury items. Most of the vessels could have served for cooking, for storage, or for eating or drinking. There is, however, more of a standardization of form, surfacing, and decoration than was seen in Xe.

San Felix pottery figurines are represented by more and better specimens than those of the Xe phase; but, insofar as we can say, they seem to be very much the same sort of little solid, turbaned, female figures. They were handmade, of course, and often slipped (usually cream). One small fragment that comes from San Felix deposits is a little monkey-head. The figurines came from both B Group and house mound proveniences.

Other San Felix ceramic items were unperforated potsherd disks made from vessel bases and, perhaps, used as jar lids. Also a number of rectangular and ovate-trapezoidal worked potsherds, including some that are typed as notched-end pendants or weights, are associated with the phase. Some fragmentary objects that are probably modelled pottery ear ornaments can be added to the San Felix list, as can an intact cylinder seal with a deeply cut, stylized turtle motif. This latter came from

20. For the details on this see Saul (1972, table 8 and text).

the Structure B-II platform, San Felix phase.

In our summary of the Xe phase we mentioned the possibility that a little monolithic red sandstone table, found in B Group, might be taken as an indication of ritual or ceremonial functions associated with that part of the site. Nine of these tables, from San Felix levels in B Group, would, indeed, seem to indicate such functions at this later date.

Other ground stone artifacts, almost certainly of a utilitarian nature, were also encountered in connection with the San Felix B Group platforms. These are metates, of the basin-shaped, turtleback form, mortars, and several varieties (thin-rectangular, thick-ovate-rectangular, plano-convex, and triangular) of mano stones. Here we run into a problem of provenience and association. Are these metates, mortar, and mano items from the B Group San Felix structures *in situ* domestic debris or fill inclusions? The metates and mortars were fragments, as were most of the manos. Our exposures were not large enough to clear sufficient floor areas of these early platforms so that we could be absolutely certain that we were dealing with *in situ* floor finds; however, on balance, and considering the amounts of living detritus found on and around these B Group platform levels, I am of the opinion that these various milling stone implements were probably once in use in B Group buildings. Such an interpretation would see domestic and ceremonial functions carried on within the same immediate precincts and, perhaps, within the same buildings.

To continue with stone tools and ornaments in use during the San Felix phase, we have recorded the following ground stone items: rubbing and pounding stones, celts (including one found with Burial 129), apparently nonutilitarian sandstone forms such as cubes, little cupstones, slabs, and scored stones, and a greenstone effigy pendant (with Burial 131). In chipped flint or chert, a number of choppers or celts were found in B Group and in the house mounds; a flint core was associated with Burial 127 and other cores came from general house mound and B Group refuse; flint nodules were used as pounders and were found in all parts of the site; and flint flake wastage was similarly distributed. With reference to the last we did not find sufficient concentrations of it in any mound or other location to suggest a flint-knapper's residence or shop. Obsidian bladelets, of the regular-notched and plain regular varieties, both with and without use-nicking, came from all parts of the site at this period.

No shell ornaments or other artifacts can be associated with the San Felix phase. In fact, the only shells in use at this time appear to have been the river mussels (*Amblema* sp.) which had been taken from the river, with limy incrustations still on them, and used in platform masonry (the *almejas*).

Bone materials came from various San Felix refuse proveniences. These included awls, punches, an eyed-needle, plain and incised tubes, a rasp-tube, a straight-headed pin, bits of worked antler, and pierced animal teeth. Most of the awls, pins, and tubes were made from deer long bones. In addition, animal bone refuse, unworked or in some cases showing cutting marks, included deer bones, a number of dog bones, and a jaguar bone (cut).

We have mentioned the deposit of *Canavalia* beans that may date as either Xe or San Felix. To this we can add, with a definitive San Felix dating, charred maize of the Nal-Tel variety.

The San Felix phase population at Altar de Sacrificios would appear to have been only slightly larger than that of the Xe phase. There were some divergences in pottery styles from the earlier phase, but there was also some continuity. Household artifacts remained about the same. More information on burial practices is available to us from San Felix than was the case for Xe, but because of the limited Xe burial evidence we can say little of a contrastive nature. The one Xe burial was in a simple pit grave and had no grave goods associated. The several San Felix burials were similar interments but were accompanied with one or two vessels and an occasional nonceramic artifact. The skeleton from the single Xe burial was that of a man who had been in good general health insofar as this could be determined from the bones. The skeletons of the San Felix individuals, both adults and children gave some indications of disease and dietary deficiencies. As we shall see, these indications of pathology continue from this time throughout the pre-Columbian history of Altar; but whether or not health conditions were better in Xe phase times than later can hardly be posited on the basis of a single individual.

The one major difference between the San Felix phase and the preceding Xe phase is seen in the architectural changes that took place in B Group. In Xe times perishable wood and thatch structures with packed clay floors had stood there. They may have been ordinary dwellings or they may have been the dwellings of community leaders. In either case, it is unlikely that they differed greatly from houses that were to be found scattered around on the western periphery of the site. In San Felix times, or at least by the end of that phase, artificial earth platforms had been constructed around what was now a formal plaza. These were faced with *almeja* and limited amounts of red sandstone masonry and had terraces and stairs. Clearly, they were special buildings of some sort. Perhaps they were platforms on which the houses of chiefs or leaders were built. While domestic debris is found in and around them, other items are found there such as little sandstone tables or benches which do not occur in the simpler earthen platforms of the house mounds of the same period. The preponderance of the evidence points to the beginnings of a politico-religious or ceremonial center.

As noted, the ceramics of San Felix can be grouped into the Mamom ceramic sphere. Thus, in its wider relationships, San Felix relates to Uaxactun Mamom (R. E. Smith 1955), to the Jenney Creek complex of the Belize Valley (Willey et al. 1965), to the Escoba complex of Seibal (Willey 1970), and to other Maya lowland Middle Preclassic complexes. To the highlands, to the southwest, its links are with Escalera and Francesca of Chiapa de Corzo (Warren 1961) and to the related Mirador III and IV phases (Peterson 1963) and those that are contemporaneous in the Santa Cruz region (Sanders 1961). On the Guatemalan Pacific coast the comparable phase would be Conchas 2 (M. D. Coe 1961). In the Guatemalan highlands I would see connections with Las Charcas (Borhegyi 1965), and there are undoubtedly ties to the Sakajut and El Porton ceramics, where we also noted earlier Xe similarities (Sedat and Sharer 1972; Sedat 1972; Sharer and Sedat 1972). There are also some ties, although of a more general nature, to the north, in Yucatan, on the lower Usumacinta, and the Tabasco and southern Veracruz Gulf coast. These have been summarized by Adams (1971; see also Willey, Culbert, and Adams 1967).

Speaking of the origins of the ceramics of San Felix Adams (1971, p. 154) states:

> In general terms, the relationships between Xe and Mamom [including San Felix] spheres are surprisingly weak, considering the apparent *in situ* development.

And he is inclined to see the Mamom ceramic complexes of the Peten as deriving from a second colonization of the southern Maya lowlands. While this is a possibility to be considered, I am more disposed to see local lowland developmental continuity as being the most important process in the rise of the Mamom pottery styles.[21] For instance, this can be observed very clearly in such traits as the monochrome surfacing of the vessels and in the various plate forms. Such an interpretation would not deny continued outside stimulation and contacts; but whether or not there was a new influx of people at this time remains to be demonstrated.

This question is, of course, a broader one than just that of ceramic innovation. What appears to be the most important change between Xe and San Felix at Altar is the rise of a more complex society as revealed in the architectural clues to corporate labor structures and a ceremonial center. Is this to be interpreted as a second colonization or as an essentially local socio-political development occurring in response to continued outside trade and other contacts with peoples who

21. In this view I am undoubtedly conditioned by my familiarity with the Seibal Preclassic ceramics and with the transition from Real Xe to Escoba Mamom at that site, which seems clearer than the Xe to San Felix Mamon transition at Altar.

were more advanced in this regard? In view of the relatively gradual nature of the changes that were to take place at Altar in the succeeding centuries, changes generally moving in the direction of increased socio-political and hierarchical complexity, I am more inclined to see this Xe-to-San Felix transformation as a segment in a course of development that was carried out by local populations in systemic adaptation to on-the-ground demographic changes, albeit within a wider context of contacts with the general cultural evolutionary changes that were going on elsewhere in southern Mesoamerica.

PLANCHA PHASE

During the estimated 450-year period (300 B.C.–A.D. 150) of the Plancha phase, Structure B-I became the most imposing pyramid of B Group and of the site. Its earliest Plancha building level, dating to the early part of the phase, is Construction F. Totaling only 3 meters in height, it immediately overlay the late San Felix Construction G. It was a clay platform floored on top with burned earth and gravel covered with plaster. There had been a wattle-and-daub building on this platform which had had interior walls of smoothed lime mortar that had been painted red. The next two Plancha levels, Constructions E and D, raised the total height of the mound somewhat. Construction E was similar to Construction F and had had a perishable summit structure. Construction D was a little more elaborate. It had been very definitely terraced and had a stairway constructed of red sandstone blocks. Both Constructions E and D also date to the earlier part of the Plancha phase. Construction C dates as late Plancha. Unlike the earlier construction levels of B-I, it had been completely faced with shell concretions or *almejas*, set in a mortar of lime, ground shell, and earth.

Construction B, the latest Plancha phase level of Structure B-I, was completed toward the end of that phase. It was a large terraced pyramid, standing at least 9 meters above the plaza floor of its time. It had been covered with an *almeja* masonry coating, much as the antecedent Construction C had been. The lower portion of Construction B, the north face of which was removed at the time of the building of the overlying Construction A, probably consisted of a square, triple-terraced platform which was ascended on the north (or plaza) side by a projecting stair of red sandstone. The upper portion of Construction B was composed of three more terraces, and these were set back toward the south edge of the lower portion of the pyramid. The lowest of these three upper terraces had on its north side a broad central stairway and two small lateral stairways. The central or main stairway was built of red sandstone blocks, a few limestone blocks, and *almejas*. The top of the next terrace was originally reached by a wide stairway of only two steps; but later, in early Salinas times, this was divided into two small stairways by a long central block. The uppermost of these three upper terraces had a small stairway centered on its north side. Quite typical "Classic" features associated with Construction B were a basal molding on the uppermost of the upper terraces and a stucco scroll design (badly battered) on the floor of the top terrace of the lower portion of the pyramid. There probably had once been a rectangular, wattle-and-daub and thatch-roof building, presumably a temple, on the topmost terrace of the pyramid. Under this topmost terrace, or Building Platform, was a dedicatory cache (Cache 45) consisting of a pottery plate. This cache had been placed on the central axis of the building.[22]

While the earlier Plancha platforms or pyramids are relatively simple affairs, Construction B is obviously coming into the tradition of the great Maya lowland pyramids or politico-religious buildings. The features of the basal molding, the stucco scroll, and the central axis votive cache are all very definitely in this tradition.

22. For more detailed descriptions, cross-section and plat drawings, and a restoration drawing see Smith (1972, pp. 73–84, figs. 29–31).

The other Group B buildings were also added to during the Plancha phase.

In the house mound area, to the west of Group B, some earlier house mound platforms were built over in the Plancha phase, and a number of new house platforms were built. Twenty-eight definite small mound occupations are tallied for Plancha—an impressive increase over San Felix—plus a few possible occupations and a number of other mounds with minor Plancha pottery occurrences. Some of the Plancha house mounds were faced with *almeja* masonry in a manner similar to that of the Group B structures.

As noted, the trait of votive caches first appears at Altar in the Plancha phase. Such caches are defined as one or more objects buried together as an offering. Ten are recorded for the Plancha phase. Seven of these were found in Structure B-I, including the one referred to in the summit building platform of Construction B of that mound. Besides this, one came from Group B Plaza; one from Mound 2; and one from Mound 7. These caches all consisted of pottery vessels, from one to seven in number. Quite probably, these vessels contained foods at the time they were placed as offerings. Obsidian bladelets, four in number, were also found in a vessel in Cache 60, and jadeite or other greenstone beads were in the vessels of Caches 37 and 44 (see Smith 1972, pp. 205–211, for a discussion of caches, and table 4 and Appendix A, pp. 235–242, for their detailed listing).

Fifteen burials were recorded for the Plancha phase. Most of these were in simple pit graves in either extended or flexed positions. But two burials were in somewhat fancier graves, one occurring in a crypt in Structure B-III and one in a stone cist in Structure B-II. Besides these locations, burials were found in Structure B-I and in house mounds nos. 2, 8, 10, 17, 18, 26, and 40. Pottery vessels were found with most burials, and jadeite and flint objects with others (see Smith 1972, table 5). An adult male (Burial 8) in Mound 2 had filed teeth (the upper central and lateral incisors).

In addition to caries and tooth loss, some of the Plancha burials showed enamel hypoplasia of the teeth, highly suggestive, as already noted, of childhood malnutrition. Instances of spongy-porotic hyperostosis cranii and osteitis are also recorded.

Substantial sherd collections, as well as whole vessel specimens from burials and caches, give us a good picture of Plancha phase ceramics. The types show continuities from San Felix. This is consistent with the ceramic history of the Peten as a whole since the Chicanel ceramic sphere, of which Plancha is a part, can, in large degree, be derived from the Mamom sphere. A diagnostic type is the polished monochrome, Sierra Red—a ceramic clearly descended from the antecedent Abelino Red and Joventud Red types of Xe and San Felix. Black and cream monochromes also persist. Incised, punctated, and fluted decorations do also; however, these plastic techniques have become less common. A very diagnostic vessel form of the phase is the medial-flange bowl.

In general, the Chicanel horizon is a time of remarkable ceramic uniformity throughout the southern lowlands, and this uniformity can be extended even to northern lowland Late Preclassic ceramic complexes. Of interest is the fact that while the Plancha phase saw a marked differentiation between domestic and ceremonial architecture, with the construction of the temple pyramid of Structure B-I, it did not record a parallel divergence in ceramics. The tomb and cache pottery of Plancha is essentially the same as the ceramics found in domestic refuse contexts. In the latter part of the Plancha phase, however, Altar began to respond to foreign influences in ceramics and, especially, more elaborate ceramics. This is seen very clearly in a positive-painted imitation of Usulutan resist-painted ware, an Altar type known as Itzan Red on Gray. Associated with this new painted style are tetrapodal nubbin feet, unbridged round spouts, banded appliqué decoration, and a distinctive multiple-line fine-incising. These foreign influences, probably deriving from the highlands (El Salvador and southeastern Guatemala), became much more clearly defined in the succeeding Salinas phase when a differentiation between what might be considered elite pottery wares and ordinary wares began to be noticeable.

As is the case elsewhere in the Peten in the

Late Preclassic Period, there is a decline in figurine manufacture in Plancha. Only a few specimens were recovered at Altar. One of these is a solid human head that appears to be in a Preclassic tradition; the others are hollow, but apparently handmade, pieces.

Large, unperforated sherd disks are in the Plancha inventory, as are small perforated sherd disks which are probably spindle whorls. These last are not as common as they are to become in later phases, but their Plancha presence is definite. There is also a continuity from earlier phases of such things as the various odd worked sherds, probably pendants, and the notched-end pendant or weight type. Pottery ear ornaments are represented by nicely made napkin-ring forms. Although figurine modelling had declined in Plancha, we found some fragments of what appeared to be small modelled effigy vessels. One of these was a miniature hemisphere with a modelled human face; the others were fragments of animals.

The basin-shaped, turtlebacked metate and a number of mano forms continue through the Plancha phase. The latter include most of the form varieties of the mano except the square. Mortar fragments are also present; and we recorded one barkbeater, the earliest Altar de Sacrificios occurrence. Other utility and nonutility ground stone items in Plancha contexts are much like those of the previous San Felix phase: rubbing and pounding stones, pebble hammers, celts, and oddly shaped worked stones (cuboids, cupstones, spheres, cylinders, and slabs). Jadeite beads occur for the first time, being associated with burials and caches, as we have indicated. They include subspherical, cylindrical, barrel-shaped, and other form varieties. All are quite small.

Plancha chipped flint implements are similar to what they had been before. The chopper or chipped celt was the most common type—in fact, the only standardized type. In addition, we found some rather irregularly shaped unifacial and bifacial scrapers, as well as nodule pounders, cores, and flakes. Several cores and large numbers of flakes came from Plancha phase refuse in Mounds 26 and 29, suggesting possible household workshops. Obsidian cores, in every case small and exhausted, were also present in Mound 26, as well as in Mound 14 and in Groups B and C. Obsidian bladelets were found in virtually all Plancha contexts. These were both of the size we have defined as regular and also of the more delicate slender variety. Obsidian flakes are also present although we did not recover many of these from any part of the site.

Shell artifacts were rare in Plancha. *Oliva* sp. shell tinklers may pertain to the phase although this is not absolutely certain. A U-shaped item, obviously carved from a large heavy marine shell, and which may be a finger-loop for an atlatl, is identified as Plancha, as are some pierced musselshells and a small, thin shell, crescentlike adorno that may have been a clothing ornament. Bone implements and ornaments were much the same as for San Felix: awls, tubes, and pins. In the bone remains the dog, ocelot, tapir, deer, turtle, and crocodile are all represented.

What may be the remains of some burned copal were found with a Plancha burial (Burial 105), a crypt burial of a young adult male placed in Structure B-III. Other than this, the only vegetal substances recovered from Plancha contexts were burned maize (Nal-Tel variety) grains.

Like the antecedent phases, Plancha is lacking in any truly monumental stonework. One of the red sandstone tables may date from this time although the provenience placement is equivocal. A large red sandstone hourglass-shaped object came from a Plancha level in Structure B-II, and a small, red sandstone monkey carving was taken from Plancha refuse in Mound 22.

In summary perspective, we see the Plancha phase at Altar de Sacrificios as a time of steady cultural buildup. This is seen in population increase, increase in trade contacts, and an *in situ* socio-political development toward a nonegalitarian society. The essential continuousness of this social development is implied in the very nature of the major buildings and their changes. The earliest Plancha temple platforms were constructed immediately upon and over the earlier architecture of the San Felix phase, and, subsequently, these mounds were added to and rebuilt at various times during the Plancha phase. By the time Construction B of Structure B-I was completed the society of Altar de Sacrificios was surely of a nonegalitarian sort, with a centralized leadership operating out of the B Group ceremonial center. Although the local Altar house mound count was higher for Plancha times than it had been before, the 28 dwelling platforms, give or take a few, that were occupied at any one time during the phase seem hardly enough to have provided the essential adult male manpower for the B Group constructions of the period. The estimated 450 years of the phase is, of course, a long time; however, it is highly unlikely that such a pyramid as Construction B, of Structure B-I, was accreted at the rate of a few loads of earth per day over that long a time. The individual mantling constructions must have been relatively rapid operations, accomplished within a dry season of a few months. The sand clay and fill that went to make such a mantling as Construction B would not have withstood heavy tropical rains from one season to another. Such soft earth would have to have been packed in and sealed over with the masonry coatings, without allowing for overlong exposure to the elements. Thus, large work gangs would have been employed for relatively short periods of time, and this bespeaks centralized labor direction.

These trends of the Plancha phase are in keeping with what was going on elsewhere in the Maya lowlands, and even farther afield, in the Late Preclassic Period. Plancha ceramics are a part of the tight-knit Chicanel ceramic sphere, and Plancha, thus, was contemporaneous and undoubtedly in contact with the Chicanel phase of Uaxactun, the Chuen and Cauac phases of Tikal, and many others of the southern lowlands. Outside of the southern lowlands there are also strong links seen with the ceramics of northern Yucatan, Chiapa de Corzo, the Guatemalan highlands, and El Salvador. Highland-lowland trade routes were active at this time, in obsidian, jadeite, and probably other raw materials. As we have seen they were also active in ceramic products. And with this trade must have passed the stimulation of ideas about institutional aspects of culture. Local growth in the lowlands, as in the Plancha phase at Altar, was vigorous, but it also proceeded in a larger setting of cultural alliances.

SALINAS PHASE

We have estimated the Salinas phase as dating from A.D. 150–450, a 300-year period more or less evenly divided between the Protoclassic and Early Classic Periods of the major Maya lowland chronology. It was a time of continued activity at Altar de Sacrificios. Structure B-I, which we saw on the *almeja* masonry-covered Construction B at the close of the Plancha phase, was redone in Salinas to assume its final form as the red sandstone-covered pyramid dominating Group B. In this final form, the pyramid, designated as Construction A, was 13 meters high, roughly square, and about 32 meters across the base. It rose in ten or eleven terraces. The basal three were similar to those of the preceding Construction B although the wide stair that had ascended these was now divided by a projecting block. The remaining seven or eight terraces were set back toward the south edge of the third terrace, much as had been the position of the upper portion of Construction B, although these upper terraces now rose more steeply than was the case with the Plancha building (compare the reconstruction drawings in Smith 1972, fig. 29). Two small stairs rose from the third to the fourth terrace of Construction A. From the fourth terrace to the summit of the pyramid was another wide central projecting stair. From the remains on top, it is likely that a low summit platform or Building Platform supported a building or temple that had low sandstone foundation walls and an upper part of pole-and-thatch construction.

The red sandstone blocks that were used in the masonry facing of the Construction A terraces and in the walls of the temple were well and evenly cut, from 35 to 60 cm in length and 20 to 25 cm in width and thickness. The soft sandstone was, of course, easy to work, and so it must have been a relatively simple task to fashion such building stones. They were carefully coursed and set in only thin mud mortar. The careful dressing of the blocks allowed for close fitting. Quite possibly, the facing of the terraces was once covered with plaster, but none remained. In some places the masonry courses were bonded; however, because of the nature of the soft clay and sand hearting material, the stones could not be tied securely to the fill. As a result, subsequent tree growths and fall, following abandonment of the site, caused much of the masonry to become disarranged.

The final building levels for Structures B-II and B-III were also of redstone and also date as Salinas phase. Both structures were pyramids, and they probably had temple-type buildings on their summits in much the same manner as Structure B-I. Structure B-IV, the larger, palace-type mound, also had a final red sandstone building phase, probably of Salinas date.

House mound or small structure occupancy in the Salinas phase does not differ greatly from that of Plancha. We counted 24 definite occupations, one probable occupation, and 14 additional mounds with scatterings of Salinas sherds. Some of the house mounds had Salinas phase terrace facings of red sandstone or limestone blocks.

Caches 8-30—either a series of separate caches or, perhaps, one great cache—were found under the main upper stairway of Construction A of Structure B-I, a late Salinas-phase offering presumably made on the completion and dedication of this construction. These caches—or this single cache—was composed of pottery vessels. Many of these had been placed lip-to-lip as though they originally had contained food or some other perishable offerings. Pottery types that are represented are late Salinas. As such, they were crucial to our dating of Construction A as terminal Salinas.

Caches 31 and 32, also lip-to-lip bowls, were found in other locations in Construction A of Structure B-I, as was Cache 38, a single pottery bowl. Cache 40, consisting of 28 large potsherd disks, was another Structure B-I cache. All of the sherd disks appear to have been burned. Cache 54 was found on a centerline position in Structure B-II and is interpreted as dedicatory to the final phase of that construction. It was a single pottery bowl containing fish bones, turtle-shell fragments, a small stone sphere, and some carbonized material. Cache 55 was from Mound 38. It also was a single pottery bowl, in this instance found inverted over a stone disk. All of these caches are dated as Salinas.

Four other caches may date as Salinas or may be somewhat later. One of these is Cache 7, which Smith (1972, table 4, pp. 236–237) places as Salinas. It was found under the big red sandstone censer altar, designated as Censer Altar A. This altar had been placed on a small platform between the two small stairs on the third terrace of Construction A, Structure B-I. There was no pottery vessel, but the cache consisted, instead, of two unperforated sherd disks, three laurel-leaf flint blades of a kind that could be considered ceremonial, three stone beads, a small pyrite disk, and a polished pebble. This totals ten items. It is possible, however, that the pebble was an accidental inclusion. Caches 5, 6, and 3 are placed by Smith in a Salinas-Ayn-Veremos time range. Two of them, Caches 5 and 6, came from under Altar 3, the large redstone altar on the plaza floor directly in front of Structure B-I (see Smith 1972, figs. 29–31). Cache 5 contained nine flint eccentrics and one obsidian bladelet; Cache 6 was composed of nine flint eccentrics and 677 pieces of obsidian (including bladelets, cores, flakes, and fragments of these). Cache 3 was found under Altar 4, a redstone altar in the center of the North Plaza of A Group. It contained 13 eccentric flints (including, as eccentrics, some laurel-leaf blades).

Four burials date as Salinas and two as Salinas-Ayn. One of the Salinas burials (No. 101) was an urn burial of a small child or infant (ca. 6 months); all others were simple pit inhumations. The urn burial and one other were in B Group; the remaining four came from house mounds. All burials (except for the urn interment) were either extended or flexed; no consistent pattern of head orientation was observed. Burial 99, of pure Salinas date, was an adult male who, according to Smith (1972, p. 260), showed pronounced fronto-occipital deformation of the cranium. Unfortunately, the cranium of this individual was not sufficiently well preserved to allow us to remove it for laboratory study, and this field observation on deformation could not be confirmed by Frank Saul. If this was a true case of fronto-occipital deformation, it is the earliest instance at the site. However, it should be noted that this burial (Burial 99) was not dated by grave pottery as none was found with it. It is placed as Salinas only from its stratigraphic context in Structure B-III. It was actually found intrusive into earlier Preclassic levels of that mound, but the grave appeared to originate from a Salinas level. Although pottery was not among the grave goods, Burial 99 was accompanied by various nonceramic items, including a shell disk adorno with iron pyrites attached, a jadeite bead, a lump of raw jadeite, a stingray spine, a bone bead, and some bits of worked *Spondylus* shell. Grave goods with the other Salinas or Salinas-Ayn burials included pottery, small shell items, and obsidian.

Salinas pottery shows continuity out of Plancha in both its utility wares (Sapote Striated would be a good example) and in its maintenance of the new pottery decorative elaborations that we remarked upon in the latter part of the Plancha phase. These new features include, and are part of a complex with, Usulutan ware. They include: mammiform tetrapodal supports (in Plancha these had been small nubbin supports), resist-painting, polychrome painting, dichrome painting, multiple-line decorative motifs, and ring-bases. Quite characteristic of the Salinas complex are several new types. One of these is a monochrome, Aguila Orange, which also carries over into Ayn. Others are Caribal Red, Guacamallo Red on Orange, Gavilan Black on Orange, and Ixcanrio Polychrome. For the first time in the Altar sequence we now see pottery which could be designated as "luxury ware," in contrast to the more ordinary household wares of the previous phases. In these finer wares Salinas pottery relates indisputably to the Maya lowland Protoclassic horizon.

Pottery figurines found in Salinas refuse contexts are few. Occasional small, solid, handmade human heads, of a Preclassic genre, may be refuse carry-overs from earlier times found out of true cultural context. More common fragments of hollow (but probably handmade) animal figurines are probably true Salinas manufactures.

Miscellaneous pottery items of Salinas include the large unperforated sherd disks, of which 28 were found in Cache 40 (see above). Perforated disks, both large and small, and presumably spindle whorls, also occur. The notched-end pendants, as well as other worked sherds that may have been ornaments, are present as well.

Modelled pottery items are earspools (probably the napkin-ring type), flat stamps, cylinder seals (although the dating is not absolutely certain), panpipes or conjoined flutes, and animal effigy vessels which are stylistically not unlike some of the above-mentioned hollow animal figurines except that they are larger.

Salinas shows no essential changes in metate or mano forms from the preceding phase, and other implements classed as rubbing and pounding stones are much the same. We found no celts; however, since they occur in earlier and later phases this is probably the result of limited sampling. Miscellaneous nonutilitarian stones of the phase are spheres (one is Cache 54), cylinders, and polished pebbles.

We have mentioned a little polished pyrite disk that came from Cache 7. If it is properly dated to Salinas then the trait of using the pyrite mirrors can be extended back this early at Altar. Jadeite beads are found in Salinas caches; and pieces of fine mosaics, while not securely dated, may also be this early.

The standard flint choppers or celts are a part of the Salinas chipped stone. Innovations at this time, however, may include the laurel-leaf flint blades and the curious eccentrics. We have referred to these from Caches 7, 5, 6, and 3 (see above). There is, however, a problem in the dating of these caches; so it is possible that these chipped stone pieces do not appear at Altar until later—that is, until the Early Classic Ayn and Veremos phases. This same ambiguity surrounds the dating of a number of other laurel-leaf and eccentric specimens, most of which came from near the surface of Structure B-I and which might be Salinas or later (see Willey 1972, pp. 156–157).

Obsidian bladelets, both regular and slender

varieties, flakes, and cores can all be identified with the Salinas phase. The huge obsidian deposit of 677 pieces that we found in Cache 6 (see above) is, as noted, only provisionally dated as Salinas. The same could also be said of the dating of the few obsidian eccentrics that we found at Altar.

Shell ornaments are, for the first time, relatively common at Altar in the Salinas phase. We found *Oliva* tinklers with Burial 134 and a composite shell and pyrite rosette with Burial 99. Marine shell was now available for making such things, and additional evidence for trade contact with the seacoast is seen in the presence of stingray spines.

Bone implements and ornaments are much the same as previously.

Some rather crude, and relatively small, red sandstone and pumice sculpture, showing graffitolike designs or portraying men and animals, may date as Salinas although the possible phase assignments of these pieces are mixed.

As to the presence of monumental stone sculpture in Salinas, the problem is essentially one of dating and of phase definitions. The earliest dated stela from Structure B-I is Stela 10 which, as we have said in our review of the Altar chronology, has an Initial Series dedicatory date of 9.1.0.0.0 or A.D. 455. We have taken this as the inception of the Ayn phase (ca. A.D. 450) so that by this definition there were no dated stelae encountered by us at Altar de Sacrificios which could be assigned to the Salinas phase. We may wonder, however, about some of the other monuments on the north face of Construction A, Structure B-I. Were they set up prior to the dedication of Stela 10, contemporaneous with the completion of Construction A? If so, they might be considered as dating to the terminal years of the Salinas phase. This is implied in Smith's (1972, p. 236) dating of Cache 7, found under Censer Altar A, as late Salinas. If correct, this would date this big sandstone altar that early. Graham (1972a, pp. 85–86), in discussing another altar from Structure B-I, Censer Altar C, has this to say about the zoomorph carved on the altar:

> The face presents grotesque serpentine/dragon motives strongly reminiscent of the Late Preclassic masks decorating the stairway of Structure E-VII-sub at Uaxactun. Functionally as well as stylistically, the piece also recalls the three great stone censer altars, or "three-pronged incensarios," of Kaminaljuyu (Monuments 16, 17, and 18), which can be regarded as surely of Late Preclassic age; the Altar de Sacrificios mask, however, is much closer in style to the Uaxactun masks, to which the Kaminaljuyu specimens also exhibit relation.

Graham goes on to note that while Censer Altar C was found associated with the butt of Stela 10 its mask is stylistically consistent with a Cycle 8 date—a dating which would place it, of course, well before A.D. 455 and within the range of our Salinas phase chronological estimate.[23] Thus, it is at least possible that some of the altars of Structure B-I belong to the Salinas phase.

In review, we see the Salinas phase at Altar de Sacrificios as a time of rapid change. If we are correct in our dating of the phase, not quite all of the elements of Maya Classic civilization had been assembled at Altar de Sacrificios by the close of the period; but many of them had been and the rest appeared very shortly afterward. There had been innovations in ceramics, especially in the direction of decorated and elaborately painted vessels. Trade connections had intensified and widened, as witnessed by ceramic products and materials from the seacoasts. Ceremonial center construction, although following along in many of the traditions established in the previous Preclassic phase, was elaborated by large-scale stone construction. New iconographic and, presumably, religious and ideological elements appeared. These are seen on the polychrome pottery and in the serpentine/dragon motif of the sculpture on the Censer Altar C. And either at the very end of the phase or soon thereafter we have the first appearances of typically lowland Maya ritual objects of

23. Adams (personal communication 1972), while agreeing that the iconography of Censer Altar C is overwhelmingly Late Preclassic or Protoclassic in its cross-ties, does call attention to a Boca phase pottery censer from Altar (Adams 1971, figs. 102, *a-c*) which is remarkably similar.

chipped flint and obsidian known as "eccentrics."

Through all of this, however, there does not seem to have been any appreciable population increase at Altar de Sacrificios. If anything, there may have been a slight decline, at least insofar as this can be measured by house mound occupance in the immediate vicinity of the ceremonial center. The manifestations of Maya hierarchical culture in the Salinas phase are, thus, not to be directly correlated with demographic changes.

Adams, in attempting to explain the Salinas innovations, feels that new peoples bringing new traits and ideas, including the essential seeds of Classic Maya civilization, appeared at Altar de Sacrificios at this time. In his words (Adams 1971, p. 155):

> The drastic nature of this replacement, it appears to me, cannot easily be explained other than by an influx of new population into Altar.

He is inclined to postulate a violent overthrow of the resident political and religious forces of the Plancha phase, with the formation of a new society in Salinas times of rulers (the invaders) and ruled (the old resident population) (Adams 1971, p. 157). That is, there was not a complete replacement but a partial one. This is, more or less, the same kind of phenomenon that Willey and Gifford (1961) had postulated for Barton Ramie in the Belize Valley at just about this same time. In Adams's opinion, the invaders and invasion are tied up to Usulutan pottery and to the other ceramic traits that are linked to the Protoclassic Usulutan horizon. He would look to El Salvador, rather than the Guatemalan highlands, as the source, and he cites the presence of Usulutan ware in Chul and Caynac complexes of El Salvador (Sharer and Gifford 1970).

Although I once shared in this idea of a Protoclassic invasion of the southern Maya lowlands in the Protoclassic as a significant event in crystallization of Classic Maya culture, on further reflection I am less convinced of it.

I think there are three instances in the culture sequence at Altar de Sacrificios when a case for alien population influx or invasion may be argued. We have already referred to one of these: the point in time of the change-over from Xe to San Felix. The second instance is the one we are concerned with now, the relatively sudden burgeoning of elite culture in the Salinas phase. The third and last is the appearance of the Jimba phase at the close of the late Classic Period. Of these three, I would consider the Xe-San Felix change-over to offer the weakest support to an invasion hypothesis. At the other end of the scale, I think that the evidence of the Jimba phase presents the strongest evidence for such a hypothesis. The Salinas case lies somewhere in between; but my present inclination is to interpret it as culture change benefitting by stimulation from foreign contacts but without actual invasion. For one thing, there was at Altar, in the Plancha phase, and earlier, a gradual buildup in ceremonial architecture. The Plancha Construction B of Structure B-I was an imposing terraced pyramid, with sophisticated architectural features, not much smaller than the Salinas phase red sandstone Construction A which covered it. This would indicate a similar kind of centralized community control for Plancha and Salinas. The architecture and the votive caches in the structure would also imply some continuity in religious ideology even though the iconography of Salinas pottery and the carving of Censer Altar C may symbolize new ideological elements. There are, however, as Adams has made clear, a number of changes in Plancha ceramics, especially those of the late facet of the phase, that foreshadow the full appearance of the Protoclassic horizon wares in Salinas. This, too, speaks for gradualism of change through trait introduction rather than forcible take-over of the site.

In addition to the local Altar de Sacrificios data, there are other things to be taken into account in our attempts to interpret the Protoclassic or Floral Park horizon. Ceramics of the Floral Park sphere have a curious geographical distribution. They are known along the eastern edge of the southern Maya lowlands, at Holmul (Holmul I phase) (Merwin and Vaillant 1932) and Barton Ramie (Willey et al. 1965); and then they occur again, in strength, only on the far opposite side of the Peten, at Altar (see Willey, Culbert, and Adams 1967). In between, at such sites as Tikal and Uaxactun, they are either missing or weakly represented. In this connection, Adams (1971, p. 158) states:

> There is no evidence of a Protoclassic period at Tikal or of the associated Floral Park Sphere ceramics. There is no doubt, either, of the essentially indigenous nature of cultural development toward the level of civilization by about the time of Christ. Therefore it should be kept in mind that when we talk of site unit intrusion [i.e., invasion] represented by Floral Park Sphere ceramics, it applies only to those sites within the distribution area of Floral Park Sphere. Outside the spatial area of this sphere other equally sophisticated developments were taking place.

In other words, the climb to the level of civilization in the southern Maya lowlands was accomplished in some places without the benefit of the Protoclassic horizon or Floral Park sphere traits which Adams sees as marking an invasion at Altar in the Salinas phase.

Clearly, we still have much to learn about the Preclassic-to-Classic transition in the Maya lowlands, and at our present state of knowledge it is best to maintain alternative hypotheses for future examination and testing. The absence of strong Protoclassic horizon or Floral Park sphere traits at some sites does not, ergo, deny the possibility of an invasion and new population influx at Altar de Sacrificios. Indeed, one could conceive of a model where sophisticated invaders took over certain sites at the peripheries of the Peten, and where these sites, in turn, served as transmission points for new ideas that were then assimilated by other sites at the core of the area and mediated by purely local leaderships. Alternatively, however, such peripheral sites might merely have been more exposed to trait intrusion from alien cultures, might have accepted more of these traits, and might have passed them on, in a moderated way, to the core sites. The first model would be closer to Adams's interpretation of the Salinas phase, the second to mine.

AYN PHASE

During the Ayn phase the politico-religious center of Altar de Sacrificios remained at Group B; and Structure B-I, as completed in its Construction A phase, must have continued as the principal temple. There was no more building on this structure nor on any of the others of Group B, with the possible exception of Structure B-IV; but a number of altars and stelae were set up on the north face platforms and terraces of B-I. These were all of red sandstone. There were five stelae in this group. All bore Initial Series dates. As noted in the previous section, the earliest is Stela 10. It had been placed on the east side of the third terrace of Construction A, in front of the small stair leading from the third to the fourth terrace (see Graham 1972a, for all details on this and other monuments). It was probably associated with Censer Altar C. The Initial Series date is 9.1.0.0.0 (A.D. 455), the approximate date at which we begin the Ayn phase. Stela 11 appears to have been erected as a counterpart of Stela 10 for it is on the west side of the third terrace, in front of the small stair on that side. It was associated with Censer Altar B. The dedication date is a katun later than Stela 10, 9.2.0.0.0 (A.D. 475). Stela 13 is next in chronological order, with a date of 9.3.0.0.0 (A.D. 495). It was placed on the west side of the masonry block that divides the lower stair of Construction A. Stela 18/F was not found in B Group, but Graham is of the opinion that it was originally dedicated here at 9.4.0.0.0 (A.D. 514) and that its position was on the east side of the masonry block, as a counterpart to Stela 13. At a later time Stela 18/F was removed from B Group to the South Plaza of A Group and a date was carved on the previously plain back. Stela 12, the latest of the B Group series of dated monuments, with an Initial Series date of 9.4.10.0.0 (A.D. 524), had been set up on the eastern section of the lower stairway of Construction A. In addition to these five stelae, Graham is of the opinion that a sixth was intended and that it would have been placed on the western section of the lower stairway, as a counterbalance to Stela 12. Its dedicatory date would have been a lahuntun later, at 9.5.0.0.0 (A.D. 534); however, such a monument was either never carved and dedicated, or, if it was, it had been moved and was not found by us.

These five Group B stelae, with their Initial Series dates, are all considered as securely within the Ayn phase as we have defined it (A.D. 450–554). In addition, there are a number of other monuments at Altar, both in Group B and elsewhere, which are best discussed at this point. Some of them may be slightly earlier than the Ayn phase; others may be a bit later; it is safest to say that they date somewhere in a late Salinas-Ayn-Veremos chronological range.

Some of these monuments, in fact, those most probably dating toward the early end of this chronological range have already been referred to in the preceding section on Salinas. Most notable among these is Censer Altar C, the red sandstone basin-altar with the serpent/dragon carving. There is a stylistic argument for a pre-Ayn date for this monument. The Uaxactun E-VII-sub masks to which it has been compared date to Cycle 8. At the same time, Censer Altar C was probably associated with our Stela 10. While I am of the opinion that the altar probably is earlier than the stela, there is a possibility that it is contemporaneous and dated to Early Cycle 9 and the Ayn phase. Another possible Salinas phase monument is Censer Altar A. Its central position on the terrace on the north side of Construction A, Structure B-I, suggested to Smith that it might have been placed there at the time of the completion of the building, that is, late in the Salinas phase. We have referred to this dating in our discussion of Cache 7 in the previous section. We have similarly referred to Altar 3 in connection with the dating of Caches 5 and 6. This altar was placed on the Group B Plaza floor in the front of Construction A. It has a weathered concentric band of glyphs around the altar top. Smith placed the caches found under it in a Salinas-Ayn-Veremos time range; Graham narrows this by dating the altar as Early Cycle 9, which would make it Ayn.

Other Group B monuments, not previously referred to, which may date somewhere within the Salinas-Ayn-Veremos range include: the third redstone censer altar, Censer Altar B, found with Stela 11; Altar 6, an oval-shaped red sandstone altar, associated with Structure B-II;[24] and Altar 7, a badly smashed redstone altar associated with Structure B-III. All of these are classed as decorated altars, since they display various degrees of carving. Several plain altars can also be added to the list: Plain Altars 15 and 16, associated with Structure B-I, and Plain Altar 14, on top of Structure B-IV. There are also Stelae 20 and 21, plain sandstone monuments, found, respectively, behind Censer Altar A and in a niche in the center of the upper stair of Structure B-I, Construction A. Finally, there are the two curious obelisks of white limestone. They are situated one on each side of Censer Altar A. Both had cross-hatched, scored decoration on their front sides.

Besides the Group B monuments, there is Plain Altar 17, on top of Structure C-II, and Plain Altar 19, on top of Structure C-I. These are of red sandstone, and very likely date somewhere in the Salinas-Ayn-Veremos range.

At the close of the Ayn phase there was a shift away from B and C Groups to the area of the site that was to become Group A. While there is a scattering of some early pottery on the old ground surface in the Group A area, the earliest platforms were constructed here either at the very end of the Ayn phase or in the succeeding Veremos phase. Construction D, a red sandstone mound with terrace and stair features, which represents the earliest building level of Structure A-III is such a platform. In connection with this shift to A Group, it will be recalled that a votive cache (Cache 3) was found beneath a red sandstone altar (Altar 4) in the center of the North Plaza of A Group and that this cache is dated somewhere in the Salinas-Ayn-Veremos time range. I think it likely that Altar 4 falls at the end of this range and is one of the earliest monuments in A Group.

House mound or small structure occupations of the Ayn phase tally as fourteen definite occupations and a half-dozen or so instances of occasional Ayn potsherd occurrences. On the face of it, this is a decrease from Plancha and Salinas occupations; however, it

24. Graham (1972a, p. 84) gives Altar 6 location incorrectly as Structure B-I.

will be remembered that those phases were estimated as being of 450 and 300 years duration, respectively. Our estimate for Ayn is only a little over a century. Thus, the interpretation of population decline during Ayn (Smith 1972, pp. 186–187) is still open to some questions. We cannot yet shade our Preceramic and Protoclassic Period ceramic dating fine enough to allow for house mound counting by 100-year intervals that would be comparable to the duration of Ayn. One thing is certain, though: there was relatively less large-scale ceremonial building in Ayn than in the two previous phases. This slackening of building may indicate population decline, although not necessarily.

To continue with other aspects of the culture of the Ayn phase at Altar, we may list votive caches, at least insofar as three such (Caches 3, 5, and 6) have been dated in the Salinas-Ayn-Veremos chronological range. These already have been described in the review of the Salinas phase.

Five burials are dated as late Ayn (as opposed to those already noted as Salinas-Ayn), and there is one placed only as late Ayn-Veremos. All of these burials are simple interments, and most of them are flexed. None shows cranial deformation, and only one (Burial 7) has filed teeth. All were from house mounds, and all the late Ayn burials are identified by their ceramic grave goods. Shell ornaments, greenstone beads, and obsidian were also found with one burial and shell and jadeite ornaments and a stingray spine with another (see Smith 1972, table 5). One burial, an adult male, showed evidences of arthritis-like lesions in his right sacro-iliac joint, his humerus, radius, and a recently healed parry fracture of the ulna; another revealed both tibial osteitis and arthritis. Caries, premortem tooth loss, periodontal degeneration, and enamel hypoplasia were also noted among the burials.

Ayn pottery belongs to the Tzakol ceramic sphere (Willey, Culbert, and Adams 1967); however, these relationships to the sphere, and particularly to Uaxactun where Tzakol has been defined, are more pronounced in late facet Ayn than in early. For Ayn in general, there are carry-overs from the preceding Salinas ceramic complex. Striated jars remain common although the type is a new one, Triunfo Striated. Both Caribal Red and Aguila Orange, prominent Salinas monochromes, are retained in Ayn. The new polychrome type of early facet Ayn is Actuncan Orange Polychrome. Like the earlier Salinas type, Ixcanrio Orange Polychrome, it is characterized by design motifs that are primarily geometric. Its typical vessel form is the Z-angle, ring-based bowl, a shape also found in the Ayn monochromes. The late facet Ayn polychrome is Dos Arroyos Orange Polychrome. This is the classic Tzakol sphere polychrome, featuring designs that are derived from life-forms and the basal-flanged bowl shape. Other late facet types are Caldero Buff Polychrome, Balanza Black, Urita Gouged-Incised, and San Roman Plano-Relief. Pottery lids are also a feature of Ayn, and in the late facet the Teotihuacanoid slab-footed, tripod cylinder jar appears (although it is rare) at Altar de Sacrificios.

According to our chronological arrangements and interpretations, the Ayn phase is contemporaneous with Tzakol 2, with, perhaps, an overlap into Tzakol 3. Such an alignment is necessary if we adhere to our stelae-association datings for the close of the Salinas phase at A.D. 450. However, as already mentioned in our discussion of chronology, there is a problem here on ceramic style alignments, with a number of similarities also seen between the early facet of Ayn and Tzakol 1 of Uaxactun. Thus, the possibility that we have dated Ayn too late must be kept in mind as an alternative. This possibility, though, does not receive full support in ceramic comparisons of early Ayn and Tzakol 1, for there are also differences between the two complexes. For example, early Ayn does not have the diagnostic basal-flange bowl which does appear in Tzakol 1 at Uaxactun. Also, early Ayn has more of a transitional appearance than Tzakol 1. It retains a great deal of Salinas whereas Tzakol 1 makes a more sudden appearance at Uaxactun, showing little of the preceding Chicanel complex at that site. Of course, at Uaxactun there is no Salinas complex nor any very substantial Protoclassic horizon complex.[25] Such are the complexities of the cross dating of Altar de Sacrificios Salinas-Ayn and the Uaxactun Tzakol phases. The matter is, obviously, not finally resolved; however, in view of some of the ambiguities in the Uaxactun Tzakol 1 and 2 separation at that site, together with the regional distinctiveness of ceramic sequences in the Peten, we are willing to accept some comparative disjunctions. Farther afield, there are linkages, although not of the solidity of the ceramic sphere relationship, with Chiapa de Corzo and Kaminaljuyu. These contacts are revealed not only in the appearances of Tzakol-like ceramics in these places but of highland traits in the lowlands in Early Classic times. Thus, at Altar, certain animal effigies and the "cream-pitcher" vessel form point to these highland relationships. It is also probable that the Teotihuacanoid vessels at Altar, although indicative of remote central Mexican inspiration, resulted from influences brought via the Guatemalan highlands.

The dating of Teotihuacan influences at Altar de Sacrificios, and in the Maya lowlands in general, deserves special comment. At Altar the few Teotihuacan-like ceramics we found fall in the late facet of the Ayn phase. This may correlate with either late Tzakol 2 or early Tzakol 3 at Uaxactun. At Tikal (W. R. Coe 1962, 1967) such Teotihuacanoid ceramics come within a period of about 9.1.0.0.0 to 9.4.0.0.0 or, at most to 9.5.0.0.0 (A.D. 455–534). Whether it is designated as Tzakol 2 or 3, we can be certain we are talking about the time just before the Classic stelae hiatus.

There are no Ayn pottery figurines. This is in keeping with Maya lowland traditions of the Early Classic Period.

Miscellaneous Ayn ceramic items include the various worked sherds. We have mentioned the large unperforated sherd disks from the caches which may date as Salinas or may be as late as Ayn. Perforated sherd disks or whorls are known from the phase and so are notched-end and other types of worked sherd pendants or weights. Modelled pottery objects, insofar as these may be identified with the Ayn phase, are much the same as in Salinas: napkin-ring earspools, panpipes or conjoined flutes, and animal effigy vessels.

Oddly, we recorded no definite Ayn metate or metate fragment; but this must be a sampling lack. In the house mounds with levels of this phase we found manos of the thick ovate-rectangular and plano-convex varieties, as well as rubbing and pounding stones.

Jadeite beads and mosaic-type adornos of jadeite and shell were encountered in Ayn contexts.

In chipped flint we have already discussed the caches of the general Salinas-Ayn-Veremos dating range which contained eccentrics and laurel-leaf blades. Almost certainly these items were being made and employed in ritual purposes at Altar in Ayn times. The same observations can be made about chipped obsidian; and, in addition, obsidian bladelets were common to the phase.

Marine shells were used for beads and, as noted, for mosaics. A composite shell and jadeite human face was found with Burial 115 in Mound 36.

A bone spindle whorl came from Structure A-III debris, and a stingray spine was found in Burial 116. Dog and deer bones were a part of Ayn refuse.

In minor red sandstone sculptures a rather crude god face (possibly Itzamna?) came from probable Ayn debris.

In general, the scant nature of Ayn artifacts probably reflects the relatively limited digging in Ayn deposits and, perhaps, the relative brevity of the period.

Let us review our interpretations of the Ayn phase, its relationships to the antecedent Salinas phase, and the relationships of both to wider events in the Maya lowlands. First, while we have seen the Ayn phase at Altar de Sacrificios as the first fully Classic Maya cultural expression at that site, we have also pointed out that many of the elements of Maya elite culture were already present there in Salinas (and even late Plancha) times. Second, we have favored an interpretation which brought Tzakol sphere ceramics to Altar at a somewhat later date than their first appearances in the northeastern Peten. Third, we

25. R. E. Smith (1955) has designated a Matzanel complex in the Protoclassic Period position at Uaxactun, but it is represented by only a very few specimens.

have placed our Early Cycle 9 stelae as contemporaneous with these earliest Altar de Sacrificios Tzakol-type ceramics and have considered both the stelae and the ceramics as our defining criteria of the Ayn phase. Fourth, we have considered that the Early Cycle 9 stelae at Altar were derived from the northeastern Peten centers. These Altar de Sacrificios stelae are the earliest Initial Series monuments on the Pasión-Usumacinta system, antedating by three to four katuns the earliest monuments at Yaxchilan and Piedras Negras. Thus, Altar was the first important ceremonial center in this whole region, although by 9.5.0.0.0 it had lost this preeminence.

Our first interpretation is fully sustained by the internal evidence at Altar de Sacrificios. Our second and third interpretations, which must be considered together, rest on the assumptions that there was a lag of a century or more in the spread or acceptance of Tzakol sphere at Altar and that the first appearance of Tzakol-type pottery was coincident with the dedication of the Early Cycle 9 stelae in B Group. We have discussed these problems at some length, and, while holding to our interpretation, admit the possibility that we may have placed the chronological boundary between the Salinas and Ayn phases a century or more too late. Our fourth interpretation, that of the derivation of the Classic-type hieroglyphs and Initial Series monuments at Altar from the northeast Peten, seems supported by the great weight of the inscriptional evidence now at hand from the Maya lowlands. To be scrupulously fair, however, we should remind the reader again of the El Porton Preclassic monument in the Baja Verapaz and of the similarity of this and other highland Preclassic monuments to the later lowland monuments. The lower Pasión and the southern Peten are the regions which lie closest to the Baja Verapaz and the highlands. It is, therefore, possible that Early 8 Cycle monuments are yet to be discovered somewhere in these regions. In this connection, Graham has said (1972a, p. 115):

> . . . it would be well to bear in mind the evidence for the destruction of the earliest carved monuments in later epochs at sites such as Uaxactun, Uolantun, and Tikal. It seems very possible that with the inauguration and spread of period-end dedication in Early Classic stela practice, many Preclassic monuments became obsolete or were subjected to iconoclastic destruction. With good reason to believe that sculpture was carved at Polol quite early (Proskouriakoff 1950, p. 110), Preclassic monument activities are brought close to the vicinity of Altar de Sacrificios.

However, we did not find Preclassic or Early Cycle 8 monuments at Altar de Sacrificios or elsewhere on the lower Pasión; and Graham, himself, has no real doubts that the monuments which we discovered at Altar de Sacrificios are of northern Peten inspiration and expresses his views on this point as follows:

> I consider the earliest surviving Altar stelae as provincial and derivative from the Tikal-Uaxactun area; I do not consider it possible that they were locally developed. If there were substantially earlier stelae (not found owing to their ancient destruction) at Altar, these might be more like those of Polol and with ties to Porton-Kaminaljuyu. (Graham, personal communication 1972; see also Graham 1972a, p. 119.)

The only possible Cycle 8 carving now known at Altar is the early Censer Altar C, but this has stronger ties to Uaxactun than it does to the Guatemalan highlands. We can only conclude by saying that if hieroglyphics and early dated monuments had their Maya lowland beginnings along the lower Pasión or in the southern Peten the discoveries to demonstrate this have yet to be made.

VEREMOS PHASE

Veremos is a phase of very brief duration, dating at some time during the Classic Maya stelae hiatus. To recall our estimates, that of Adams is the single katun from 9.6.0.0.0 to 9.7.0.0.0 or from A.D. 554 to 573, while Smith has placed it slightly later at A.D. 570–585. We have already noted that at the very end of Ayn, or perhaps in Veremos, building activities were shifted to A Group. Some of the interior platforms of the A Group structures were built at about this time. One of these is Construction D of Structure A-III. Built of red sandstone blocks, with terrace and stairway features, it dates as either terminal Ayn or initial Veremos. Construction C, the designation given to some additions to Construction D, is similarly dated. In Structure A-II there is also the possibility that the earliest building level, Construction D of that mound, is Veremos, although here the possible dating range is Veremos-Chixoy. This, too, is a red sandstone, terraced platform, with stairs on its east or plaza side. On its summit were platforms that may have been bases for altars. At its foot is Stela 19, a plain sandstone monument, that was probably accompanied by the sandstone table altar, Plain Altar 9. If the dating on Construction D is Veremos, this is an interesting occurrence of a stela, albeit a plain one, during the hiatus. If, on the other hand, Construction D dates as Chixoy, the monument was probably not set up during the 9.5.0.0.0 to 9.8.0.0.0 hiatus. Still another possibility of a Veremos structure is the small inner core mound of Structure A-I. In this instance, the immediately overlying Constructions D of Structure A-I are Chixoy and early Pasión, respectively.[26]

Only six house mounds show definite Veremos occupation, with one doubtful occupation and five appearances of minor sherd occurrences in other mounds. This is less than half of the occupation tally of house mounds in the preceding Ayn phase. If our estimates of the brevity of the phase is correct, this might be no more than a function of elapsed time, but a population decline is a possibility.

The only caches which we discovered that might be referred to the Veremos phase are the three (Caches 3, 5, and 6) that have been discussed under the Salinas phase and that can be dated no more precisely than a Salinas-Ayn-Veremos range.

Eight burials, however, were tabulated for Veremos and two for Veremos-Chixoy. These were all simple inhumations, flexed or extended, without any consistent head orientations. Five of the pure Veremos burials came from A Group structures, and one each was found in Mounds 38, 36, and 20. The two identified as Veremos-Chixoy were in Mound 2. All but one of these ten burials were accompanied by pottery vessels of Veremos or Veremos-Chixoy types so that phase identification is reasonably secure. Jadeite ornaments were found with three burials, one in Structure A-III, one in Mound 38, and one in Mound 36. The burial in Mound 38 (Burial 112) had filed teeth; the one in Mound 36 (Burial 114) had pyrite-inlaid teeth. The skeletons from most of these burials showed conditions of bone and dental pathology similar to those of the previous phases (e.g., osteitis, arthritis, spongy-porotic hyperostosis, caries, periodontal degeneration, and enamel hypoplasia).

Veremos ceramics retain some Ayn types, such as Triunfo Striated jars, although the Veremos version of these jars can be distinguished by higher necks and bolstered rims. The Tzakol sphere type, Dos Arroyos Orange Polychrome, also continues; however, a new polychrome type, Saxche Orange Polychrome, makes its first appearance. It is characterized by interior, rather than exterior, bowl decorations, by naturalistic animal designs, symbolic scenes, and hieroglyphic band decorations—all traits which appear transitional into the Tepeu styles of the Maya Late Classic. Similarly, in vessel form the basal flange is modified in Veremos to only a small basal ridge. Shallow tripod plates appear. A monochrome type, Subin Red, also comes into the Altar sequence for the first time. This type, in its several varieties, is to continue on through the Late Classic Period at Altar. The more strictly Teotihuacanoid vessels are no longer in evidence; however, a residue of this tradition is seen in some use of slab-footed tripods. A distinctive type, Japon Resist, is a good Veremos marker.

On the wider ceramic scene, the Veremos complex finds some close parallels in the Uaxactun Tzakol 3 subphase, especially in things like the tripod polychrome plates and the type Japon Resist, as well as in plano-

26. In Smith (1972, p. 113) there is a passage that says that Construction C of Structure A-I is Veremos. This is an error that occurred in rewriting. As far as Structure A-I is concerned, only the inner core mound has any chance of being Veremos. Construction C of A-I is early Pasión phase.

relief decoration and vessel wall fluting of cylinder jars; however, Veremos has more continuity with the ensuing phase at Altar, Chixoy, than Tzakol 3 shows with its Uaxactun successor phase, Tepeu 1. We suspect that Veremos probably correlates with very late Tzakol 3-very early Tepeu 1, and this is borne out by the fact that Tzakol 3 at Tikal is defined as the time of purest Teotihuacanoid influence (W. R. Coe 1962) while at Altar de Sacrificios, as we have said, the peak of this influence is past by Veremos times.

It is just possible that moldmade pottery figurines appear as early as Veremos at Altar; but it should be emphasized that this is uncertain. We have tabulated one fat-face type figurine from A Group as being in Veremos refuse; but this may have been intrusive from a later midden.

As might be expected, our Veremos artifact sample is extremely small. Perforated sherd disks (whorls) can be identified to the phase, as can the notched-end pendants or weights. The napkin-ring earspool may be present; and we did find fragments of what appear to be small effigy vessels, similar to those of earlier phases.

Metates (of the turtleback kind) are present, as are manos (thin-rectangular variety), rubbing stones, and celts. In chipped stone, there can be little doubt but that laurel-leaf blades and eccentrics were present, in addition to the ubiquitous chipped celts. Obsidian bladelets and flakes can be added to the list.

Overall, we can say that Veremos, at Altar, was a time of transition, from Early Classic to Late Classic patterns. This is seen especially in ceramics. It was not a major building period although some new temple and/or palace-type constructions were erected. These were placed some distance away from the previous ceremonial structures of the site, and they formed the beginning of what was to be the main plaza arrangement of buildings in the full Late Classic Period at Altar. There may have been a population decline at Altar in Veremos times, perhaps a continuation of one that had begun in Ayn, although our data do not tell us this unequivocally. It was certainly a period of little or no stelae activity, or a period from which little sculpture has survived—a circumstance matched elsewhere in the southern Maya lowlands during this same time.

CHIXOY PHASE

Red sandstone continued as the building material through the Chixoy phase. Construction E of Structure A-I was made of blocks of this material, and the redstone Construction D of Structure A-II was of either Veremos or Chixoy date, as we have already indicated. No other building levels were identified definitely as being of Chixoy date although it is possible, or even likely, that some of the smaller platforms surrounding the South Plaza of A Group were built at this time.

Three redstone stelae from the South Plaza of A Group must date from either Chixoy or early Pasión. Adams has estimated the Chixoy dates as A.D. 573 to 613, or 9.7.0.0.0 to 9.9.0.0.0; Smith's estimates are A.D. 585 to 630. If Adams is correct, then the three stelae in question are just pre-Chixoy while if Smith's estimate is closer to the mark they could be considered Chixoy. The earliest is Stela 18/B. This, it will be remembered, was a monument that had been dedicated at a much earlier time in B Group; but, subsequently, it was moved to A Group, where it received additional carving and was rededicated. Its new dedication date is 9.9.5.0.0 (A.D. 618), the earliest Initial Series date at Altar after the hiatus. It was found on the east side of the South Plaza, near Structure XIX. Stela 8, the next of the three in chronological order, was found at the north end of the South Plaza, near Structure A-XVII. Its date is 9.9.15.0.0 (A.D. 628). The last of these three stelae, Stela 9, came from the south end of the South Plaza, on Structure A-XXIV, and it has the date 9.10.0.0.0. (A.D. 633). The problem of their phase placement is one of architectural and ceramic associations; and it is not easy to resolve these to give a clear Chixoy or Pasión date. What limited ceramic data we have from Structures XIX and XXIV (see Smith 1972, pp. 68–71) support a Pasión rather than a Chixoy placement;

however, it is best, for the present, to leave this fine-line chronological and phase assignment in abeyance.

One thing is interesting in the placement of these three stelae (see Graham 1972a, p. 116). It will be noted that there is no monument for the hotun ending 9.9.10.0.0. If there was such a monument one would expect it to be found on the west side of the plaza, the only side without a stela. This would have completed a symmetrical dedication pattern characteristic of the Classic Maya. We did not find such a monument on the surface of the site; but our excavations on the western side of A Plaza were extremely limited, and it is possible that such a stela is to be found there below ground.

These three stelae, with their associated red sandstone altars, imply that the South Plaza of A Group may have been the principal ceremonial focus of Altar de Sacrificios in Chixoy-early Pasión times, prior to the building of the large Pasión phase structures of the North Plaza and the dedication of later stelae there. Still, there were some red sandstone monuments in the North Plaza at this relatively early time, or, perhaps, even earlier. We have mentioned Stela 19 and Plain Altar 9 as having been associated with Construction D of Structure A-II, a building dated as Veremos or Chixoy. To this, we should also add Altars 1 and 4. Altar 1 is the famous "namesake altar" at Altar de Sacrificios. It was found on an upper or Pasión phase level of Structure A-II, but both Graham (1972a, pp. 75–78)[27] and Smith (1972, p. 49) are of the opinion that it was carved earlier and that its original association was with Construction D of A-II. Altar 4, it will be remembered, is the red sandstone altar found in the center of the North Plaza of A Group. It was associated with Cache 3, and both were dated somewhere in the Salinas-Ayn-Veremos time range. Graham (1972a, pp. 82–83) remarks upon its similarity to Altar 1 and suggests that the two are contemporaneous.

27. Graham places it as prior to 9.10.0.0.0, as opposed to Morley's earlier estimate of "9.15.0.0.0 ???". In a recent (1972) note to me Graham has stated that he feels Altar 1 to be related to Stelae 18/B, 8, and 9 on epigraphic grounds and, therefore, of their chronological period (9.8.0.0.0–9.10.0.0.0).

In house mound occupations Chixoy shows a slight increase over Veremos, with eight definite occupations, three probables, and eight or nine additional instances of minor Chixoy pottery occurrences in other mounds.

Only a single votive cache (Cache 52) is dated to Chixoy. This came from Mound 36 and consisted of only two Chixoy pottery vessels.

Five burials date as Chixoy, two as Chixoy-Pasión. Of this total of seven, four were found in Structure A-I, and three were taken from the "burial mound," Mound 2. All were simple inhumations. Most of them were found in an extended position. Pottery was the most usual grave artifact although shell ornaments were found with one Structure A-I burial. Another Structure A-I burial had filed teeth. None showed any definite signs of cranial deformation. Smith had indicated this as a possibility, based on his field observation of Burial 55; however, Saul did not confirm this. The latter notes traces of spongy-porotic hyperostosis in this same individual as well as periodontal degeneration in another burial of the phase.

Chixoy ceramics are defined by new varieties of Saxche Orange Polychrome (Saxche and Sabalo), by restricted orifice, round-sided polychrome bowls, and by increased occurrences of tripod polychrome plates with the designs on the insides of the plates. A smudged-interior tripod plate is also a common type (Zopilote Smudged Black). There are also plastically decorated vessels (Ojo de Agua Incised and Silkgrass Fluted) as well as massive occurrences of red monochromes (Subin Red: Bocul variety and Tinaja Red). These last include a bolstered rim caldron form and other jar forms.

The wider relationships are clearly with the Tepeu ceramic sphere (Willey, Culbert, and Adams 1967) and with the Tepeu 1 subphase as seen at Uaxactun and Tikal. There are, however, regional differences separating Altar from the northeast Peten. These have been formalized in varietal differences in the ceramic typology, in both the polychromes and in the Subin Red group. There are Altar similarities, too, with Piedras Negras, especially in bowl forms, and Adams notes parallels between the Copador polychromes of Copan and the Altar Saxche Orange Polychrome type.

While the phase assignments are somewhat equivocal, it is likely that the first moldmade figurines of pottery made their appearance in Chixoy. These were probably types that could be included under what Butler (1935a) has called "Style Y." It is not until later, however, in the Pasión phase, that we have definite documentation of the occurrence of moldmade figurines at Altar.

As was the case with Veremos, our sampling of Chixoy deposits is relatively limited; therefore, the absences of such things as perforated sherd spindle whorls should not be taken too seriously. As we have seen, these occur earlier, and they also occur later at Altar. Napkin-ring earspools were found in Chixoy contexts as were small animal effigy vessels.

Chixoy ground stone includes metates, manos, barkbeaters, rubbing and pounding stones, stone pendants, and jadeite and other stone disk-shaped beads. This is the earliest occurrence at the site of the disk-form head, as opposed to the tubular or subspherical variety. Ring-stones or doughnut stones also make a first appearance in Chixoy.

In chipped flint there are also innovations, with the first site occurrences of the tapered-stem group of projectile points. Celts or choppers continue, of course, as do laurel-leaf blades. These last include large ceremonial forms, but there are also other smaller ones which are not so finely chipped and which could have served as utility points or as knives.

There are also flint eccentrics. Simple tools include drills, scrapers, and pebble choppers. The range of obsidian artifacts includes bladelets, cores, and flakes.

Disk beads appear in shell, as well as in stone; and in bone we have tubes, spatulas, and at least one bone spindle whorl.

Some minor red sandstone sculptures are probably of this date, including a very small censer altar, a curious large wedge-shaped form found in Structure A-I, as well as some other pieces. Some of these may be detritus carry-overs from earlier periods. This would seem to be so in regard to a few fragments of the little red sandstone tables, a type found in numbers and as complete specimens in the Middle Preclassic contexts of B Group.

We have in Chixoy a consolidation or completion of the transition in ceramic polychromes that we saw in progress in the preceding phase. Chixoy fully establishes the Tepeu ceramic tradition at Altar and pertains most specifically to the Tepeu 1 horizon. There are also other artifact introductions that presage the common types of the succeeding Pasión phase: moldmade figurines, large stemmed projectile points, and ring-stones. The stelae cult probably was revived at this time, and it reappears in a more typically Late Classic form—that is, with larger stelae, emphasis on portraits, and long noncalendrical glyphic texts. Only the materials at Altar are still atypical, with a continuing use of red sandstone. This was to change very shortly, however, with the introduction of limestone stelae and altars and the replacement of sandstone by limestone in building materials.

PASIÓN PHASE

Pasión was a major building phase at Altar de Sacrificios. Most of Structure A-I, the great platform and acropolislike building at the north end of the North Plaza of A Group, was built at this time. Constructions D, C, and B all definitely date from the phase. Of these, the earliest, Construction D, was of red sandstone; Construction C was a mixture of sandstone and limestone; and Construction B was the first all-limestone platform. Its terrace walls were laid up on a batter, with the limestone blocks placed against a hearting of clay and limestone scrap, to give a much stronger type of construction than the antecedent sandstone masonry. The limestone block walls were plastered over and, in many cases, painted.

In Structure A-II, Constructions C and B, both of limestone masonry, date from the Pasión phase. The Construction C platform had seven projecting stairways on its east, or plaza, side. Although limestone was now in use as the only masonry material, it is probable that the red sandstone altars of the earlier

Structure A-II building phases were reset on the summits of the later constructions. The masonry techniques were the same as those described for this phase in Structure A-I. Walls were similarly plastered, and floors were laid with lime scrap grouting covered with a smooth surface of plaster.

Construction B in Structure A-III also dates as Pasión. It, too, was of limestone, as was the overlying Construction A. However, this latter construction was subsequently modified, with some mixed limestone-sandstone additions in the Boca phase and, probably, again in Jimba times.

The other major structure of A Group, the ball court on Structure A-V, was most probably built in Pasión times. This is an open-ended court, the standard Late Classic Period type of the southern Maya lowlands. It consists of two ranges, a playing alley, and benches sloping upward to the playing walls of the ranges. The masonry of A-V is of well-dressed limestone blocks. Potsherds found on the buildings and in the court were overwhelmingly Boca and Jimba in date; however, the sherds of the fill of the ranges were Pasión so it is most likely that the court was built in that phase, even if it continued in use in later times.

Other test excavations in A Group gave further evidences of Pasión phase building, especially in Structures A-XIX and A-XXIV of the South Plaza and the court bounded by Structures A-I, A-VII, and A-VIII.

The Pasión phase was also the time of the greatest monument activity at the site. While we have considered the three red sandstone stelae of the South Plaza of A Group, Stelae 18/F, 8, and 9, as being either Chixoy or Pasión, there can be little doubt but that the next monument in order of Initial Series dating, Stela 4, belongs with the Pasión phase. It is of limestone, the earliest limestone stela with an Initial Series date at the site; it was found in association with the Pasión phase Construction B of Structure A-I; and its dedication date is 9.10.10.0.0 (A.D. 642). Stela 5, which was paired with Stela 4, on the south (or plaza) face of Construction B, was dedicated at 9.11.0.0.0 (A.D. 652). Also of limestone, it is very similar to Stela 4. Neither is a typical stela. They are best described as hieroglyphic wall panels. They have no portraits but are wholly glyphic; however, there can be no question that they are period ending markers. Also associated with Construction B of Structure A-I are two other glyphic panels (Sculptured Panels 1 and 2).[28] These are essentially contemporaneous with the stelae, both dating at 9.10.11.13.0 (A.D. 644). None of these monuments associated with Structure A-I, which date its Construction B phase to the decade A.D. 642–652, was accompanied by an altar.

In chronological order, the next stelae of the Pasión phase are those associated with Structure A-II, on the west side of the North Plaza of A Group. Stela 1 can be correlated with Construction C of A-II. It has an Initial Series date of 9.11.10.0.0 (A.D. 662). A limestone monument, like all of those dating after 9.10.10.0.0, it was carved on all four sides, with a human figure on the front. No markers for katuns 9.12.0.0.0 or 9.13.0.0.0 are definitely known for Structure A-II or elsewhere at Altar de Sacrificios; however, it is possible that one or both of these, or perhaps others with intermediate hotun endings, are buried within Structure A-II. There is also the possibility that Sculptured Panel 4 and Stela 3 were dedicated during this time. The former is a glyphic panel fragment which was found on the east or front slope of Structure A-II, near the location of Stelae 1. Its constructional associations are uncertain. Stela 3 is a badly eroded monument which was probably carved with a human figure or figures in addition to a very brief glyphic text. It was found on the east side of Structure A-II, near the northwestern end of that mound. Plain Altar 10 was in association with it. Its material, size, and shape all suggest a post-9.10.0.0.0 date, and both Morley and Graham suggest the possibility of a 9.13.0.0.0 dedication although this is a guess. The last stela associated with Struc-

28. It should be noted that on Graham's (1972a, fig. 1) plan the designations for Sculptured Panel 1 (S.P. 1) and Stela 5 are reversed. On the other hand, the positions of Stelae 4 and 5 relative to their accompanying panels have been corrected in Graham's map from the situation shown on the Bullard site map (Willey and Smith 1969, fig. 4).

ture A-II is Stela 7 which was located near the south end of mound. It has a portrait figure and glyphic text on the front, and it can be assigned the period ending date of 9.14.0.0.0 (A.D. 711). Associations are believed to be with Construction B.

No definitely dated monuments were found in association with Structure A-III; but three dated stelae are situated in the middle of the North Plaza of A Group. The earliest of these is Stela 17. This is a Giant Ahau monument, and its 4 Ahau reading has its most acceptable interpretation at 9.15.0.0.0 (A.D. 731). It was associated with Plain Altar 11, and it is the most westerly of the three North Plaza stelae (see Graham 1972a, fig. 1). The next monument in this west-to-east alignment across the plaza is Stela 16. Although very badly eroded, it had a portrait figure and an inverted-L glyphic caption on the front and glyphs on the back and sides. It was clearly an Initial Series monument, and Morley interpreted the date as 9.10.?.?.? (ca. A.D. 633). Graham, on the other hand, is inclined to see it as having been dedicated at 9.16.0.0.0 (A.D. 751).[29] Its central position in the alignment, between monuments dating at 9.16.0.0.0 and 9.17.0.0.0, supports this latter interpretation. Stela 16 was associated with Plain Altar 12. Stela 15, the most easterly of the three plaza stelae, has an Initial Series date of 9.16.18.5.1 (A.D. 769) from which a dedicatory date of 9.17.0.0.0 (A.D. 771) is reckoned. It is badly preserved, both as to its front carving (a portrait?) and the glyphs on the sides. It was associated with Plain Altar 13. The Initial Series date of Stela 15 is the latest Initial Series date at Altar de Sacrificios.

In addition to these dated monuments and their associated altars, there are a number of other monuments in A Group which most probably date from the Pasión phase. All of these are limestone altars (see Graham 1972a), and they include Plain Altar 7 (a huge altar at the south end of the South Plaza), Altar 5, and Plain Altar 18 (found on top of Structure A-III), and Plain Altars 1 and 3 (found on the top of Structure A-II).

In résumé, all of the monuments that can be definitely placed in the Pasión phase at Altar de Sacrificios are of limestone and are associated with the limestone architectural building period of the site. The earliest of these is dated as 9.10.10.0.0 (A.D. 642), the latest at 9.17.0.0.0 (A.D. 771).[30] All are in a group. Those dating from 9.10.0.0.0 to 9.11.0.0.0 are associated with Structure A-I. These are all glyphic panels rather than true stelae, in spite of their Initial Series dates. The monuments from 9.11.10.0.0 to 9.14.0.0.0 are associated with Structure A-II. Most of these are standard Late Classic stelae, with portraits and associated dates and texts. The exception is a fragment of a sculptured panel similar to those of Structure A-I. The stelae dated from 9.15.0.0.0 to 9.17.0.0.0 are in the center of the North Plaza, and these include two typical Late Classic stelae and one Giant Ahau stela.

In commenting on the nature of the texts of all of these Group A monuments of the Pasión phase Graham observes that they contain numerous chronological statements and lunar texts and that the Uniform base is used in moon counting. They also incorporate many names and titles; but in none of the Altar texts are inaugural dates and initial dates signaled by the characteristic phrases cited by Proskouriakoff for Piedras Negras and elsewhere although Sculptured Panels 1 and 2 carry inaugural notation. Graham is uncertain, however, whether this is a function of the fragmentary condition of many of these Altar monuments or whether it indicates a different system of notation (see Graham 1972a, pp. 90 and 118).

Outside of the ceremonial center of the site the Pasión phase is marked by a sharp upswing in the number of house mound occupations as opposed to the previous phases. There are 22 definite mound occupations, one questionable occupation, and seven other instances of minor Pasión phase pottery occurrences.

29. Smith (1972, table 2) gives the Morley reading.

30. Smith (1972, p. 113), in discussing the "Limestone Architectural Period" at Altar de Sacrificios, states that all definitely associated stelae dates fall in the seventh century A.D. This should read seventh and eighth centuries A.D. However, the context of Smith's discussion at this point was that of the transition from red sandstone to limestone architecture, and for this transition it is true that only the seventh century is involved.

Eight votive caches are placed as Pasión phase. One of these (Cache 2) came from under Stela 16, in the North Plaza of A Group. It consisted of obsidians. Another (Cache 48) was under an altar associated with Structure A-III. It had obsidians and eccentric flints—a total of 18 items. Four caches (Nos. 34, 35, 36, and 43) came from Structure A-I and consisted, variously, of flints, obsidians, shell, jadeite, and stingray spines. An additional cache (No. 56) in Structure A-III was composed of shell, jadeite, and stingray spines. Cache 59, in Structure C-I, consisted of a single pottery vessel.

Thirteen Pasión and four Pasión-Boca burials were divided about evenly between A Group and the house mounds. Most were simple inhumations although there was one cist burial and one crypt burial in Structure A-III. Skeletons were both flexed and extended. Grave goods included pottery and other artifacts although several Pasión burials had no accompanying objects of any kind. The most spectacularly rich burial was that of a middle-aged (40–44 years) female, Burial 128, who had been placed in a crypt in Structure A-III and was accompanied by 15 pottery vessels, jadeite, shell, flint, obsidian, and stingray spines. This particular individual also had jade-inlaid teeth, and the cranium showed tabular-oblique, fronto-occipital artificial deformation. Burial 96, a younger (25–29 years) female in a cist grave in Structure A-III, also had jade-inlaid as well as filed teeth and a similarly deformed head. This lady was accompanied by four vessels—one the handsome polychrome cylinder jar known as the "Altar Vase" (see Adams 1971, frontispiece)—and jadeite and flint artifacts. Still another female, this one of middle-age, who had been interred in Structure A-I, also had the tabular-oblique deformed head. In this instance there were no grave goods.

Bone pathology for the Pasión burials was similar to that of the earlier phases. Saul observed incidences of spongy-porotic hyperostosis, osteitis, and arthritis, as well as periodontal degeneration, abscesses, caries, premortem tooth loss, and enamel hypoplasia. There was some indication that these pathologic conditions were no respecters of persons. Assuming that an individual such as the one in Burial 96 was a person of high status (as adjudged by grave goods, artificial head deformation, and dental inlays), it is of further interest to note that this same female showed signs of spongy-porotic hyperostosis, osteitis resembling modern syphilis or yaws, and arthritis.

The elaborate polychrome pottery of the Pasión phase is consonant with the Tepeu 2 polychrome elaboration of the southern Maya lowlands as a whole. Figure painting both on cylinder jars and on bowl interiors was at its height at this time. The type Saxche Orange Polychrome continued, and the types Palmar Orange Polychrome and Zacatel Cream Polychrome made their appearances. An important bichrome type was Uacho Black-on-Orange. Positive and resist painting was also combined on some polychromes. Diagnostic form features included notched and terraced basal ridges on tripod bowls, ladle censers, and wide-flanged censers. In the Pasión early facet the most frequent monochrome types were Subin Red and Tinaja Red; in the late facet a new type, Ejercito Red appears, and this type, with its very fine or temperless paste, may have been influenced by the fine paste wares being made at about this time on the lower Usumacinta.

While the Pasión pottery complex at Altar is clearly within the Tepeu ceramic sphere there is also some tendency toward regionalization. This tendency grows more pronounced from early to late Pasión and continues on into the succeeding Boca phase. It is seen especially in red monochromes. At the same time, the intersite and interregional linkages in the fine polychrome wares continue; and at Altar we can see very specific ties to other great Peten centers. As an example, Adams (1971, pp. 59–78, 159–161) is convinced that many of the handsome polychrome and other vessels found in Burials 96 and 128 were gifts or trade pieces, brought from such centers as Yaxchilan, Piedras Negras, and Tikal by visiting aristocrats who were probably relatives of the great lady in Burial 128. Viewed in this light, such elegant pottery becomes a material sign of the growing class differentiation of Late Classic Maya society.

By the Pasión phase Teotihuacan influences

on Maya ceramics had been long dead, but there are very definite clues to continued Guatemalan highland-lowland relationships. For instance, certain Pasión phase gouged-incised types are much like those of the Alta Verapaz, and a Pasión ladle-censer appears to have had a highland origin. In return, the dissemination of Tepeu sphere polychrome painting ideas has long been recognized in the Alta Verapaz.

Numerous moldmade pottery figurine-whistles and fragments of these came from Pasión refuse deposits. These included types of both the Butler (1935a) "X" and "Y" styles. Subject matter embraced animals (turtles, frogs, monkeys, jaguars, peccaries, owls, and others), men (priest figures, warriors, individuals with elaborate or fan-shaped headdresses, and individuals with simpler coiflike, basket-shaped, roachlike, and animal headdresses), women (with rectangular-frontal hair arrangements, with center-parted hairdos, and with broad-brimmed hats), and grotesques (gods, demons, fat-faces, and old wizened faces). One type, designated by us as semi-solid, simply-dressed, is a subdivision of Butler's "Style Y," and there were some indications in the stratigraphy that it was an early Pasión type in contrast to later Pasión types that were more like the Butler "Style X." These figurines came from both A Group and from the house mounds; however, especially large deposits of them were found in some of the house mounds. For instance, Mound 24 was particularly well represented in Pasión phase figurines, and substantial numbers were also found in Mounds 25, 38, 2, 7, 8, 10, and 11.

Most of the moldmade pottery figurines are actually whistle-figurines; but, in addition to these, there are also pottery artifacts that are more strictly whistlelike in their overall form. Some of these are completely plain; others bear small human or bird-effigy adornos. A number of such whistles were found in Pasión phase contexts, including the Mound 24 mentioned above.

Miscellaneous pottery objects of the Pasión phase included many of the items seen in earlier phases; unperforated sherd disks, small perforated disks or whorls, perforated sherd pendants, notched-end pendants or weights, and napkin-ring earspools. In addition to all these, we have first appearances of such things as flare-type ear ornaments and large hollow pottery beads. Such ear ornaments and beads were found with the richly furnished Burial 128. The beads had been coated with a green stucco, presumably to give them the appearance of jade. A pottery mask, somewhat smaller than life-size, was also associated with this burial, and it, too, had been similarly stucco coated. A number of flat pottery disks (not sherds) came from the same burial. Each of these had a tiny central hole. It is possible that these are especially made spindle whorls although they may be beads, of a flat rather than a hollow-sphere type. Miniature effigy vessels also date as Pasión.

Metate fragments and near-complete specimens were found in abundance in Pasión contexts. Most of these were of the basin-shaped, turtleback type. But a new class of metate appears for the first time. This is a thin, flat form. Some of these (or perhaps all) flat specimens have legs. Others are legged (three legs) and have a bordering groove around the edge of their grinding surface. Manos are also found in great numbers. Some of these are of forms found earlier in the Altar sequence; but one variety which was not previously seen becomes the most common form of all in the Pasión phase. This is a mano with a very definite square cross section and pointed, cigar-shaped ends. These square variety manos are much more carefully fashioned than the other varieties (thick-ovate-rectangular, plano-convex, triangular, etc.).

Barkbeaters are present in Pasión, as are celts, stone spindle whorls, and ring-stones. The latter occur in large numbers and were found in both A Group and in the house mounds (as in Mound 24).

The discovery of well-furnished burials in the Pasión phase—such as Burial 128—has provided us with a relatively large inventory of luxury goods for the phase. For example, the slate-backed pyrite mirror is such an item. We have mentioned the special ceramic goods (flare-type ear ornaments, the mask, and stucco-covered beads), and to these we can add jadeite beads—of disk, cylindrical, and subspherical forms—and jadeite adornos.

Lumps of raw jadeite were also found in Pasión phase caches (Nos. 56, 34, and 48).

Chipped stone celts and chopper-pounders are known from the Pasión phase, and stemmed flint projectile points become relatively common for the first time. The most typical form is a large point, presumably a spear or lance head, with a tapered stem; however, some straight stem points occur as well as a fishtailed type. Small laurel-leaf-shaped points are also common in Pasión, and a good many of these appear (from their relative thickness and frequent breakage) to have been utility points rather than ceremonial blades. Additional flint utility types are thick bipointed knives, thick, round-based knives, and unifacial and bifacial scrapers. Ceremonial or ritual chipped flint is seen in a continuance of the thin, finely flaked laurel-leaf blades and in eccentrics. Such items are most usually found in caches. Flint scrap occurs in quantity in refuse, especially, in some of the house mounds, suggesting workshops; however, the largest deposit of flint flakes was obviously a ritual one, between 8,000 and 9,000 occurring with Burial 128.

Projectile points were also made out of obsidian at this time. These are relatively few, however, in contrast to those of flint. We found both expanded stem and laurel-leaf forms in caches. Cores are also present in caches, as are eccentrics. Bladelets continue, as in previous phases, to be the most common obsidian item at Altar. Obsidian flakes are not commonly found in refuse, although they do occur occasionally.

Marine shells are represented in the Pasión phase by disk beads probably cut from either *Spondylus* or conch shells, by rosette-type adornos, various pieces of cut or drilled *Spondylus*, and tinklers of *Oliva* and *Jenneria*. Shell ornaments were found with burials.

Stingray spines came from burials and caches, and fish vertebrae and crab claws were also found in caches. Perforated animal teeth were also recovered as burial accompaniments. Bone awls, and probably tubes and pins, came from refuse. Deer and peccary bones were also present in refuse, presumably as food remains.

A plain-plaited mat impression was exposed under Burial 128.

Charred maize (Nal-Tel variety) was recorded from refuse deposits.

Finally, a number of Classic Maya-style panels of bas-relief carving occurred as minor red sandstone sculptures. These came mostly from the ceremonial center sections of the site. Both their style and provenience indicate a Late Classic and, probably, a Pasión phase date.

The picture of Altar de Sacrificios during the Pasión phase is, thus, one of a thriving, active ceremonial or politico-religious center. Platforms and palaces and a ball court were constructed in A Group. Quite probably, some ritual activities still took place in the older, Early Classic B Group center although no additional building was done on this part of the site. The stelae cult, with its time-counting and other calendric functions, as well as its historical, commemorative, and status-validation functions, was vigorously pursued; and in these stelae activities the Altarians were a part of the larger southern lowland Maya world, participating in the calendric fashions and innovations that were being developed at this time throughout the area. This larger participation also extended to other aspects of culture—pottery and artifacts and trade and exchange in both raw materials and manufactured items. These external contacts continued to include the highland areas to the south as well as the sea coasts of the Gulf, the Caribbean, and, probably, the Pacific. Finally, all of the evidence at Altar, whether of internal development or of external relationships, points to the Maya society of the Pasión phase as being an aristocratically controlled one, in effect, a segment of Maya Late Classic society at the time of its zenith in the seventh-to-eighth centuries A.D.

BOCA PHASE

The Boca phase at Altar de Sacrificios has been dated at 9.17.0.0.0 to 10.4.0.0.0 (A.D. 771–909) (or, with the Smith estimate, at A.D. 780–900). By most archaeological reckonings, this would correspond to the latter part of Tepeu 2 and all of Tepeu 3. At Altar it was neither a time of important ceremonial building nor of stelae activities.

In A Group, the last major renovation of Structure A-I, designated as Construction A, is either late Pasión or early Boca. Some still later minor constructions on this platform are either of late Boca or of Jimba date. In Structure A-II, Construction A must be similarly placed as either late Pasión or early Boca. The rather shoddy final construction on Structure A-III is either Boca or Jimba. The ball court, Structure A-V, was, presumably, in use although there is no evidence that it was added to or rebuilt during the Boca phase. On a court bordered by A-I, A-VII, and A-VIII, and on Structures A-I and A-XIX there are signs of Boca houses having been built—and in one instance burned—but no indications of large masonry construction.

One stela, Stela 2, with a Giant Ahau date is the only monument that Graham attributes to the Boca phase. He places it at 10.1.0.0.0 (A.D. 849). It was found in the North Plaza of A Group, between the earlier Stelae 3 and 19, and was probably dedicated there well after a general cessation of monument activity at Altar de Sacrificios.[31]

But while ceremonial center construction and monument carving activities were minimal in the Boca phase, house mound occupation was not. In fact, this phase sees more of the domestic platforms built and occupied than at any other time in the site's history. There are 36 such definite occupations and two additional mounds with minor occurrences of Boca pottery.

Four votive caches date as pure Boca phase, two as Boca-Jimba. Of the pure Boca caches, one (Cache 1) came from Structure A-X and consisted of a pottery vessel and 670 flint flakes; another (Cache 46) came from Structure A-III and was composed of 16 pottery vessels; the remaining two were in Mounds 15 (Cache 51) and 24 (Cache 53) and consisted of two vessels each. The two Boca-Jimba caches (Caches 47, 50), from either Boca or Jimba architectural levels of Structure A-III, were composed of obsidians.

Twenty-one burials are identified as being clearly of the Boca phase. Most of these were simple inhumations although one cist grave is recorded; and most were flexed although some were extended. Filed teeth were noted in one instance. One adult male showed tabular-erect, fronto-occipital cranial deformation; another had tabular-oblique deformation. A third burial, a female, may have had a fronto-occipitally deformed skull. Pathologic lesions seen in the bones are generally similar to those of the preceding phases. Thirteen of these pure Boca burials were accompanied by Boca phase pottery, with vessels per grave ranging, usually, from one to four; however, one individual (Burial 88), found intrusive into Structure A-III, was acompanied by 18 pots, as well as shell, jadeite, and obsidian. This individual was one of the adult males with an artificially deformed head. Jadeite and obsidian were found with another Structure A-III intrusive burial, and obsidian occurred with one house mound burial; other than this, there were no grave goods.

Twenty additional burials are dated as Boca-Jimba. None of these had pottery, or any other artifacts, associated in the grave—a circumstance making for our joint or ambiguous phase identification. All came from either Structure A-I or Structure A-III. All were simple inhumations, generally at superficial depths and in proveniences that could be either Boca or Jimba. The greater part of them were flexed burials, and there is a predominance of head-to-east placement. As this head-to-east orientation of the skeleton is also characteristic of the subsequent Jimba phase, it may be that the larger part of these Boca-Jimba burials are actually of the Jimba phase; however, in the interests of accuracy and caution it is best to tabulate them as we have done. Five of these burials showed filed teeth. Four display definite fronto-occipital deformation, two males showing the tabular-erect variety, two females the tabular oblique. Two other individuals may, possibly, have had deformed skulls. Bone and dental pathology, of the kinds previously noted, characterized virtually all of the adult skeletons.

31. Morley originally read Stela 2 as 9.14.10.0.0 (A.D. 721) (see Smith 1972, table 2); Graham (1972a, pp. 13–15) challenges this and feels that the Giant 5 Ahau on the monument is the period ending 10.1.0.0.0.

Boca ceramics were found stratigraphically above Pasión ceramics in Structure A-I and elsewhere; however, no clearcut vertical stratigraphy was obtained on the relationship between Boca and Jimba. There were, though, instances of pure Boca deposits, without Jimba admixtures, in some localities of the site, and vice versa. That is, horizontal separations of the two complexes obtained; and these, together with the typology of the Jimba complex, and the wider relationships of this typology in Mesoamerica leave little doubt but that Jimba is later than Boca.

The Boca ceramic complex is marked by a general decrease in polychrome types and by a simplification of those polychrome types that do continue. Abstract designs replace life-form figure-painting. The diagnostic polychrome type is Anonal Orange Polychrome, and additional late facet Boca polychromes are San Isidro Orange Polychrome and Lombriz Orange Polychrome. The Zopilote Smudged Black type continues over from Pasión, but the Boca variety is distinguished by modelled tripod feet. In red monochromes the type Ejercito Red, which made a first appearance in the Pasión phase, becomes numerically more significant, but the other Pasión phase red types, Subin Red and Tinaja Red, also continue. There are some incised types (Cameron Incised and Chocc Incised) and impressed decoration (Pantano Impressed) appears in strength. Heavy folded rims and pattern striation characterize the unslipped utility wares. Finally, in the latter part of the Boca phase Fine Orange and Fine Gray pottery types appear as trade wares.

In extra-site cross-matching of Boca complex ceramics we have good parallels at Uaxactun where the late Tepeu 2 types are closest to early Boca and the Tepeu 3 types nearest those of late Boca; however, as emphasized in the discussion of Pasión ceramics, there is also notable regionalization. In fact, this is most marked on a Tepeu 3-late Boca level than earlier so that the various fluted and plano-relief types of Uaxactun are missing or rare at Altar while the red monochromes of the latter differ from those of the northeast Peten. There are Boca similarities with Benque Viejo IV and San Jose V, in central and northern British Honduras, as well as linkages with Lubaantun in southern British Honduras, and with the Chacalhaaz and Tamay complexes of Piedras Negras on the Usumacinta. In general, one has the impression that Altar de Sacrificios in its Boca phase, as well as Seibal in its related Bayal phase, is establishing a new network of connections at this time, with decreasing contacts with the northeastern Peten and its adjacent portions of British Honduras and increasing relationships with the Usumacinta and the Gulf coast. These Usumacinta-Gulf coast contacts are seen, especially, in the Fine Orange and Fine Gray pottery types. They belong to the Fine Orange Y Group of types (or Altar Group as it has been called more recently) as opposed to the Z Group (or Balancan Group) of fine paste wares (see R. E. Smith 1958 and R. E. Smith and Gifford 1965, 1966). Significantly, these Fine Orange and Fine Gray types that appear to mark the late facet of the Boca phase are either the same or very closely related to the types that define the succeeding phase at Altar de Sacrificios, the Jimba. All of these Fine Orange and Fine Gray types from both Altar de Sacrificios and Seibal have been shown through neutron activation analyses (Sayre, Chan, and Sabloff 1971) to be made in the same source area, presumably somewhere in the Gulf coast-lower Usumacinta country. In other words, there is the very high probability, if not the certainty, that the Fine Orange-Fine Gray pottery of the late Boca phase, and the succeeding Jimba phase, was made elsewhere than at Altar de Sacrificios or on the lower Pasión and that it was traded or brought into that site and region from a considerable distance.

The phasing of artifacts for the Boca phase presents something of a problem at Altar for it is frequently difficult to distinguish, on the basis of provenience and also on the basis of typology, between Boca and the succeeding Jimba. Hollow moldmade figurines are common to both phases. Most of these of the Boca phase are of Butler's "Style X" and show a direct continuity out of the earlier Pasión figurines. A great variety of human and animal forms are represented; and, if anything, such figurines are more common in Boca than previously. But there are a number of fine paste figurines of similar style as well as other fine paste figurines which are stylistically different and which we have assigned to a Jimba Group. Possibly, all such fine paste figurines, and especially those of the Jimba Group, date entirely to the Jimba phase; but, as fine paste influences characterize the latter facet of the Boca phase, it is equally possible that they, along with some Fine Orange vessels, are trade pieces into late Boca.

In addition to the small standard figurines or figurine-whistles, a few very finely sculpted large figurine heads were found in Boca contexts. Stylistically, these large heads are very definitely in the Late Classic Maya tradition.

Besides figurines, flutes ornamented with duck, bird, monkey, and human effigy features belong to the Boca phase, as do some plain whistles.

In miscellaneous pottery objects, we have both unperforated and perforated (spindle whorl) sherds, notched-end pendants or weights, and other worked sherds. For the first time specially made pottery whorls appear, as well as the perforated sherd type. There are also pottery beads, of elongated-pendant and hollow-sphere types, pottery rattles, earspools, and miniature effigy vessels. Of note, too, is the first sign of phallicism in art at the site. We found a phallus modelled of pottery (as well as two in ground stone).

In ground stone the metates of the previous phase—both the basin-shaped or turtleback type and the newer flat and legged type—continue in Boca. All varieties of manos also appear, but, as in the Pasión phase, the square-section variety is the most common. A fragment of an overhang-type mano also turned up in Boca-Jimba refuse. This is a type which demands a flat, rather than a basin-shaped, metate.

Other types in ground stone include bark-beaters, all sorts of rubbing and pounding utensils, celts (of the very small, small, and medium varieties), spindle whorls, numerous ring-stones, and large, heavy grooved stones that may have served as canoe anchors. Non-utility stones include spheres, cylinders, phallic forms (as noted above), and other more amorphous items.

In jadeite, the Boca and Boca-Jimba collections include disk, cylindrical, and subspherical beads and carved ear ornaments or adornos. These were not particularly numerous, and many of them came from the same provenience, the richly furnished Burial 88.

Chipped flint projectile points of the Boca and Boca-Jimba proveniences are much like those of the preceding Pasión phase. The large tapered-stem points are the predominant type, and both finely chipped and somewhat more coarsely worked laurel-leafs are also numerous. A few straight-stemmed and expanded-stem points are present, as well. Choppers, chopper-pounders, scrapers, and various knives are all much as before. Eccentric flints, however, are rare, only an occasional one turning up in refuse. The caches of eccentrics, noted for earlier phases, seem to have been no longer in vogue. Of interest, however, is the cache of 670 flint flakes (Cache 1); and, of course, cores, nodules, and flakes were found in several house mound refuse contexts.

Obsidian is as abundant in the Boca phase as ever. There are a few projectile points, including expanded-stem, straight-stem, and tapered-stem types, as well as a stemless example. Bladelets come from refuse, caches, and burials. We tabulated a few refuse cores and flakes, but no eccentrics came from any provenience.

Less shell appears to have been available for ornaments. A little pipe-shaped earplug was found with Burial 88, and other pins, spatulas, tubes, rasp-tubes, beads or whorls, fishhooks, worked antler tines, and pierced teeth came from various proveniences of Boca or Boca-Jimba date. There was also a good bit of refuse bone: deer, peccary, turtle, and dog. Probably significantly, and in keeping with the diminution of shell, there were no stingray spines.

Some fragments of minor red sandstone sculpture were found in Boca-Jimba collections. These included such things as the little stone tables, which are almost certainly much earlier manufactures (see the Preclassic phases) only incidentally included in late debris used as fill. Some relief panels and glyphic carvings are definitely Classic Period, but whether they belong to Boca and/or Jimba is more questionable. The same can also be said about some anthropomorphic sculptures and a jaguar head carving from Structure A-III.

In summary, the Boca phase at Altar de Sacrificios shows a slackening in public or ceremonial building and a marked decline or virtual disappearance of the stelae cult. It also shows a waning in the manufacture of, and trade in, fine quality polychrome pottery and other luxury goods. In all of these things what was going on at Altar appears to parallel what was happening at many other southern lowland Maya centers during Tepeu 3 times. At the same time, Altar shows some differences. In spite of the constructional, hieroglyphic, and general esthetic decline, there was no population drop-off comparable to that occurring at other Maya centers. On the contrary, the Boca phase may have been the most populous period on the lower Pasión. Altar also underwent a realignment or shifting of its previous interregional contacts. During the earlier phases of the Classic these had been strongest with the northeastern Peten and adjacent sections of British Honduras; but in the Boca phase these contacts shift and become especially strong with the west and northwest, that is, with the Usumacinta drainage and the Chiapas-Tabasco lowlands and the Gulf coast.

They are seen most clearly in the appearance of Fine Orange and Fine Gray trade wares in the latter part of the Boca phase at Altar. These fine paste wares are the forerunners of the succeeding Jimba phase occupation of Altar de Sacrificios. This Jimba tradition in fine paste pottery is essentially alien to the Peten Classic Maya culture although it may have been developed by Maya-speaking peoples of the lower Usumacinta-Gulf coast region. Significantly, it is a tradition with a strong Mexican or Toltec-like cast to it.

At this point, let me digress to say that the whole question of foreign intrusions into the lower Pasión Valley in Terminal Late Classic times is a much more complicated one than an hypothesis advanced some years ago by Sabloff and myself (Sabloff and Willey 1967) can accommodate. In that earlier formulation we attempted to account for the Non-Classic Maya, Mexicanoid features of both Altar de Sacrificios and Seibal by a single invasion of the lower Pasión by peoples from the Gulf coast-Usumacinta region. Adams was in disagreement with this interpretation for he felt that the presence of Fine Orange and Fine Gray pottery in the late Boca phase at Altar was best explained by trade with a Non-Classic Maya group who were located somewhere in the Chiapas-Tabasco lowlands (Adams 1971, pp. 161–165). According to his thinking, this group were the ancestors of the Jimba people who, a century or so later, then did conquer and occupy Altar de Sacrificios. I am now inclined to go along with Adams's interpretation of these events. Moreover, discussions among Adams, Sabloff, John A. Graham, and myself have led the four of us to elaborate a more all-embracing hypothesis by which to explain foreign contacts on the lower Pasión in Late Classic and Early Postclassic times. According to this hypothesis, there were two intrusions into the lower Pasión Valley. The earlier of these originated in the southern Yucatan Peninsula. These people came from the Rio Bec region, and they were represented there by the Late Classic Period buildings and sculptures of such a site as Becan (personal communication, E. W. Andrews, V, and J. W. Ball 1972). Their culture showed certain Toltec-like elements. They established themselves at Seibal perhaps as early as the end of Cycle 9; and they were responsible for the monuments at that site which Graham (1972a, 1973) has described as belonging to the "Non-Classic Facies A" group, best represented by the five stelae associated with Temple A-III (Willey and Smith 1967) and dating at 10.1.0.0.0 (A.D. 849). The later intrusion came from the Gulf coast country of Tabasco and adjacent Chiapas. The peoples of this intrusion were related to those of the first in that both had cultures which showed a fusion of Maya and Mexicanoid (Toltec-like) traits. These second intruders were the ones who traded the Fine Orange and Fine Gray ceramics into Altar de Sacrificios in the late Boca phase at the beginning of Cycle 10 (ca. A.D. 830). Eventually, their influences, probably via actual emissaries, arrived at Seibal; and their monuments at that site, which are the ones that show an increasing Mexicanization, are dated at 10.2.0.0.0. (A.D. 869) and 10.3.0.0.0. (A.D. 889), and are placed by Graham in his "Non-Classic Facies B." However, these people did not actually invade and occupy Altar de Sacrificios until the Jimba phase which we have dated as after 10.4.0.0.0 (or A.D. 909). Whether or not they invaded Seibal in the same manner is uncertain; no full Jimba ceramic complex has been found at that site; however, as stated, they made their influence felt there in the final decades before the abandonment of that center (see also Adams 1972; Sabloff 1973).

JIMBA PHASE

The Jimba phase is placed chronologically at a few decades after A.D. 900. Adams estimates it as from 10.4.0.0.0 to 10.6.0.0.0 (A.D. 909–948), Smith from A.D. 900 to 950.

We have already observed that there may have been some superficial building on Structures A-I and A-III in either Boca or Jimba times or both; however, if there was any platform construction in the ceremonial center in Jimba times it was relatively minor.

In the house mound area, to the west of the ceremonial groups, we counted nine house occupations, one questionable occupation, and from six to nine instances of minor Jimba pottery occurrences on other mounds. This is a substantial decline in small structure occupation from Boca times, even conceding the Jimba phase to have lasted only one-half to one-third as long a time. It is to be added, however, that great quantities of Jimba pottery were found superficially in A Group, and it may be that flimsy dwelling structures were placed here.

Two Jimba votive caches were recovered. These were both pottery vessels; in fact, it is only from ceramic typology that we can be certain of their phase identification. One came from Structure A-III, the other from B Group Plaza.

We placed 24 burials in the Jimba phase. All but five of these were in A Group, for the most part intrusive into the earlier structures. The five exceptions all came from Mound 2, a small mound located close to the Altar ceremonial center and one which had been used as a burial place during many of the preceding phases. All 24 were in simple pit graves. The flexed position of the skeleton was most common, and the head of the individual was most frequently oriented to the east. Over half of them had pottery accompaniments—from one to three vessels in each grave—and this helped greatly in our Jimba phase assignments. For the eleven in which no pottery was found the phase placement was more difficult and is more tentative. With one burial (Burial 82), two obsidian bladelets were found in association; with another (Burial 92), a small laurel-leaf flint point was found. Five of the burials in Structure A-I had fronto-occipitally deformed crania; one of those in Structure A-III also had an artificially deformed skull. We noted three cases of filed teeth and one of pyrite inlays (see Smith 1972, table 5, for associations of these features). As in previous phases, incidences of bone and dental pathology (of the various kinds already referred to) were high.

As we have already made clear in the Boca phase discussion, the ceramics of the Jimba tradition represent a break with old Maya Classic Peten modes and usher in a series of fine paste types. In the Jimba phase virtually all of the pottery, both utilitarian and otherwise, is of Fine Orange or Fine Gray ware. Fine Orange types of the Altar Group are: Altar Orange, Tumba Black on Orange, Pabellon Molded-Carved, Trapiche Incised, and Cedro Gadrooned. The closely related Fine Gray series includes: Tres Naciones Gray, Poite Incised, and Alta Gracia Gadrooned. Characteristic vessel forms are grater-bowls, open bowls, flaring-necked jars, and tripod forms. There are no polychromes, and, except for the simple black geometric painting on the type Tumba Black on Orange, decoration is in mold-impression combined with carving, incision, or gadrooning. The most complicated motifs occur on the molded-carved types, with designs combining naturalistic and abstract elements. Some of the iconography is reminiscent of the Tula Toltec style, but Maya motifs and Maya hieroglyphs are also incorporated into the decoration.

As has also been emphasized, the origins of Jimba pottery are placed somewhere in the Chiapas-Tabasco lowlands, or to the north and west of Altar de Sacrificios. And from the nature of the pottery we have hypothesized this context of origin to have been in a culture that had absorbed and synthesized elements of both a Classic Maya and a Toltec-like tradition. As argued, its first spread to Altar and the lower Pasión is believed to have been through trade and contact during the latter half of the Boca phase. In the Jimba phase proper, the Jimbans are viewed as an invading people who took over and occupied Altar de Sacrificios. Adams (1971, pp. 161–165) has suggested that such a Jimba invasion probably moved from lowland Chiapas-Tabasco to the Usumacinta River and from there downstream to Yaxchilan and Piedras Negras and upstream on the Pasión. Perhaps Altar de Sacrificios, at a major river junction, was a key point in this action. After a few decades, however, the Jimbans abandoned Altar de Sacrificios.

The Jimba style Fine Orange paste figurines give us some idea of the appearance and dress of the invaders. The individuals represented appear to be different physical types from the old local Classic Maya. Judging from these figurine portraits, head deformation was not practiced, and the physiognomy is that of a person with a straight forehead, short straight nose, and prominent chin. This may have been something of an idealized type, however, for the physical anthropological data (see Smith 1972, table 5, as well as Saul 1972) indicate that some Jimba burials showed either tabular erect (three) or tabular oblique (three) cranial deformation; and, of these, some can be definitely placed as Jimba by the pottery associated in the graves. This group included both men (Burials 52, 62) and women (Burials 57, 61). Perhaps some local Maya remained in the Jimba community, or it may be that some of the invaders practiced cranial flattening even though they did not reproduce it in their figurines. The costumes and hairdress of the Jimba figurines also show differences from those seen on typical Classic Maya figurines. The Jimba peoples, both men and women, wore their hair long, hanging at shoulder length. The upper part of the body, of both sexes, was often represented as nude, with a single gorget or ornament hung from the neck over the chest. Other Jimba figurines—a relatively high percentage—depict warriors, some with quilted armor or clothing suggestive of central Mexican warrior costumes. Not all warrior figurines at Altar can be attributed to the Jimba style and phase; however, a high proportion of figurines in the Jimba style depict this theme.

Besides the pottery and the figurines—both of which are highly distinctive and easy to sort from the early Boca materials—it is difficult to specify artifacts that are definitely Jimba. Perhaps the clay and stone phalli, which come from Boca-Jimba contexts, are actually Jimba imports, a clue to a phallic cult introduced into the lowland Maya area by the invaders. But, in the main, the nature of our data allows us to do no more than to indicate that Jimba weapons and utility items, and perhaps nonutility items as well, were much the same as those described for the Boca phase.

POST-JIMBA

A very few pieces of pottery are described by Adams as probably dating from after the Jimba abandonment of Altar de Sacrificios. Two sherds of Plumbate pottery are the most distinctive of these. They appear to be of the Tohil type and, as such, would pertain to the Postclassic Tohil pottery horizon which probably dates ca. A.D. 1000–1100. Less distinctive, but quite different from any of the pottery of the preceding phases, are a tripod comal and a crude flaring-sided tripod bowl (see Adams 1971, p. 109, fig. 74). It seems likely that these few pieces were dropped at Altar by casual occupants at some time after the Jimba abandonment.

III

COMMENTS ON ETHNOHISTORY AND ARCHAEOLOGY

FROM THE CLOSE of the ninth century A.D. until modern times much of the southern Maya lowlands was deserted. The great Maya Classic Period ceremonial centers—Tikal, Uaxactun, Yaxchilan, Piedras Negras, and Altar de Sacrificios (as we have described in detail)—were abandoned and not reoccupied. There were, however, some exceptions to this abandonment and desertion of the area. The well-known Postclassic Period settlement at Lake Peten Itza was a going concern when the Spaniards visited it in the sixteenth century; and there were Postclassic settlements to the east of Lake Peten Itza, such as Topoxte (Bullard 1970), Macanche (Bullard 1973), and the New Town phase occupations of the Belize Valley (Willey et al. 1965; Bullard 1973). But most pertinent to our interests here were the communities of the Chontal Maya, who occupied the territory along the western and northwestern margins of the southern Maya lowlands. These Chontal Maya were in this position in early historic times, and it is likely that they were there earlier. Quite possibly, they were involved in events at Altar de Sacrificios and in the general region of the lower Pasión Valley in Terminal Late Classic and Early Postclassic times.

That the Chontal Maya were involved with the late phases of occupation at Altar de Sacrificios, and elsewhere on the Pasión, is the thesis of J. E. S. Thompson, who has offered a historical reconstruction of this branch of the Maya lowlanders based on both ethnohistory and his interpretations of the archaeology (Thompson 1970). The historic period document which has been Thompson's principal source for this reconstruction is known as the *Paxbolon Papers*. It was translated and made available some years ago by F. V. Scholes and R. L. Roys (1948), and Thompson has devoted a major portion of his book, *Maya History and Religion,* to an ethnohistoric-archaeological interpretation of this document. According to this interpretation, the Chontal Maya, or Putun Maya, as Thompson prefers to call them, had their ancient homeland in southern Campeche and in the delta country of the Usumacinta and Grijalva Rivers of Tabasco. Their principal site or center, at least in late pre-Columbian times, was at Potonchan, probably near the mouth of the Grijalva. In this location the Putun, although of Maya language stock, were peripheral to the Classic Period Maya of the southern lowlands and probably also to those of the northern lowlands. While their earlier archaeological background must remain highly speculative, it can be reasonably inferred that by Late Classic times they had assimilated a number of Mexican-like traits from the peoples of post-Teotihuacan central Mexico and Veracruz. In early historic times these Putun also had a reputation for being great traders and great canoeists. They are said to have controlled trading traffic along the lower Gulf coast-Yucatan Peninsula shore, and it is also likely that they similarly dominated the major rivers such as the Grijalva and lower Usumacinta. Just how far back in the past these Putun maritime and riverine trading activities can be extended is a matter for conjecture; but, given the wide distribution of the fine paste wares—Fine Orange and Fine Gray—it is, again, a most reasonable surmise that Putun long-distance trade was thriving in the latter part of the Late Classic. We have already noted the presence of these fine paste wares in the Altar de Sacrificios late Boca phase, in the Bayal phase of Seibal, and elsewhere. That the Chontal or Putun Maya were the makers and distributors of these fine paste wares is supported by the fact that the center of origin of this kind of pottery, especially the Fine Orange ceramic of the Altar or Y Group, would appear to have been in the heartland of Putun territory. Significantly, also, these Fine Orange and Fine Gray wares of the Terminal Late

Classic bear design elements that show a synthesis of Maya and Nahuat iconography, a fusion of traditions that is consistent with the Mexicanoid cast of Chontal Maya or Putun culture.

In Thompson's opinion, the Putun began to expand southward and eastward, into what was then Classic Maya territory, at the close of the eighth century A.D. This may have been largely by trading activities at first, but military and political power soon followed trade. Thompson believes that they first dominated Yaxchilan. A few decades later they were at Altar de Sacrificios, and by A.D. 850, at least, they were at Seibal and Ucanal.

It is also a part of Thompson's reconstruction, although not one that immediately concerns us here, that this trade-and-military expansion also took them along the coast of the Yucatan Peninsula to Cozumel Island, which they held as a base, and that from there they pushed inland to take Chichen Itza by A.D. 918. This last move, according to Thompson, was the first Mexicanoid-Maya invasion of Chichen, one that was not accompanied by the distinctive Tula cult of Topiltzin Quetzalcoatl or Kukulcan. A second Putun wave then arrived at Chichen at about A.D. 987, and it was this group that is to be identified with the followers of Quetzalcoatl and with the Tula Toltec art and architecture for which the site is famous.

But to return to the lower Pasión Valley, Thompson wants to link the Jimba phase at Altar de Sacrificios and the early 10th Cycle monuments at Seibal to these Putun conquests. He sees the invaders as being responsible for the local revival of the stelae cult at Seibal. He does not attribute the Classic collapse to them; but, instead, the collapse, which followed after 10.3.0.0.0 (A.D. 889), is attributed by him to a "proletarian" or peasant revolt which brought old resident Maya and new Putun leadership down together. To continue with this reconstruction, Thompson considers the reported sixteenth-century Putun-speaking groups at Tenosique, downstream on the Usumacinta below Altar and Yaxchilan, as an ethnohistoric residue of this earlier Putun invasion. Also, according to the early accounts, the Putun had established themselves as the nation of Acala, or Acalan, in the region south of the Pasión, where, presumably, some of them went after their conquests. Here, it is believed, they mixed with resident Chol Maya to become the Lacandon who had a "capital" at Dolores, on the Rio Lacantun, in 1695.

Thompson's reconstruction of the Putun and their relationships to archaeologically recorded events on the lower Pasión has been reviewed and criticized in print by two of my colleagues in the Altar de Sacrificios and Seibal excavation programs, J. A. Sabloff (1971) and R. E. W. Adams (1973). Adams has been especially critical. On methodological grounds he has cautioned about the projection of sixteenth-century ethnic and linguistic distributions back in time to a period 700 years earlier, and he has questioned the wisdom of identifying the Putun as the makers of Fine Orange and Fine Gray pottery. He also has taken issue with Thompson's chronological bracketing of the Altar Jimba complex and the Cycle 10 stelae at Seibal. According to Adams's dating, the Altar Jimba phase falls after 10.3.0.0.0 while the Seibal stelae are in the 10.1.0.0.0 and 10.2.0.0.0 period. The ceramic associations of the Seibal stelae are with the Bayal phase of that site which is contemporaneous with Altar de Sacrificios late Boca, not Jimba, the Jimba phase being unrepresented at Seibal.

As this debate between Thompson and Adams is closely related to our archaeological interpretations of terminal Late Classic and Early Postclassic events at Altar de Sacrificios it deserves some comment here. In this connection, the reader should refer back to what we have said in our discussions of the Boca and Jimba phases (pp. 52–58); however, the matter is worth some repetition. In doing this, it is only fair to Thompson to point out that he was following the tentative interpretations of the prehistory of Altar de Sacrificios and Seibal, and the Fine Orange pottery influx into the lower Pasión Valley, which Sabloff and I had outlined in a preliminary article (Sabloff and Willey 1967). As has been made clear in the above discussion of the Boca and Jimba phases, we have now modified our views somewhat from those of the 1967 article and have brought them more into line with those of Adams which were made fully explicit only in the latter's 1971 monograph on the Altar de Sacrificios ceramics.

As of now, our preferred interpretation of foreign influences impinging on the Classic Maya culture of the Pasión Valley sees two sets of these influences. The earlier of these arrived in late Boca times. It is best represented by the stucco reliefs and the earlier stelae at Seibal. These belong to the group that John A. Graham (1972a, 1973) has designated as "Non-Classic Maya Facies A" at that site. They date from the end of Cycle 9 through 10.1.0.0.0 (A.D. 849). As the term "Non-Classic Maya" implies, they embody some foreign elements of design, elements which, in a general way, may be referred to as "Mexican-like" or "Toltec-like." Interestingly, many of these elements, especially as seen in the Seibal stuccos on Structure A-3 (Willey and Smith 1967), are very similar to stuccos from the site of Becan in the Rio Bec region of southern Campeche. There they are dated no later than the Tepeu 2 horizon (personal communication, E. W. Andrews, IV, 1972), or somewhat earlier than at Seibal. In other words, a case could be made out that Seibal came under the influence of peoples from Becan, or peoples related to those of Becan, early in the ninth century A.D. These may have been Chontal or Putun Maya, and the 10.1.0.0.0 stelae at Seibal are among those which Thompson identifies as Putun.

To continue with our interpretation, we visualize a second set of influences as coming into the lower Pasión Valley from the lower Usumacinta-lower Grijalva region. This second set of influences may have been a continuation of the first; certainly the two sets of influences were related. Both display "Non-Classic Maya" iconography. At Seibal John Graham has identified these influences in what he has called the "Non-Classic Maya Facies B" stelae at that site. These date from 10.2.0.0.0 and 10.3.0.0.0, and they incorporate still more "Mexicanoid" elements. At Altar de Sacrificios these influences are seen in the Fine Orange and Fine Gray decorated pottery of the Altar Y or Altar Group ceramics; and they are also seen in fine paste figurines from that site. They date from the late Boca phase at Altar, and at Seibal some of this Fine Orange pottery is also present in the Bayal phase. Shortly after 10.3.0.0.0 (A.D. 889) Seibal is abandoned, and at about this same time the Boca phase at Altar comes to an end. The succeeding Jimba phase at Altar dating from about 10.3.0.0.0 or 10.4.0.0.0[32] is represented by a pure Fine Orange-Fine Gray ceramic occupation. The site no longer appears to have been an important ceremonial center in this final phase of its history; but it would appear to have been held as a settlement and, probably, a strategic river junction outpost by a Non-Classic Maya people.

Now I do not see our interpretations of these events of the Terminal Late Classic and Early Postclassic Periods of the lower Pasión Valley as totally irreconcilable with those of Thompson. We are more immersed in, and concerned with, archaeological detail and relatively fine sequence shading than he was in his reconstruction; but I am more inclined than Adams to accept the Putun or Chontal Maya as the people who made the fine paste wares and brought them into the lower Pasión and also the people whose influences are represented in the "Non-Classic Maya Facies A and B" stelae at Seibal. Allowing for all the inherent difficulties in projecting ethnic and linguistic identifications of a historic era back into earlier centuries, I still think that the probabilities are very high indeed that the alien influences with which we are concerned are to be attributed to the Putun or Chontal. These were the people who occupied the northwestern periphery of the southern Maya lowlands in the sixteenth century; there is a very good chance that they were there earlier. This is the region of the origin of fine paste ceramics. These Putun while not having a Classic brand of Maya culture were not totally unrelated to them, either linguistically or culturally. In this geographically and culturally marginal position they were ideally located to mediate Mexican or early Toltec influences from the west, combining these with local traditions, and passing them on, and eventually carrying them on, to the Maya of the Peten.

32. Graham (personal communication 1972) is disinclined to see Jimba as quite so late and would prefer to date the phase from 10.2.0.0.0.

In this position the Putun would also have been well placed to imitate and further develop Mexican trading and military practices and to use this acquired knowledge to their own benefit and to the detriment of that of their Classic Maya kinsmen. Their relatively late florescence, coming at the time of the Maya Classic decline, does, indeed, suggest a "Macedonian" type role for the Putun, as Thompson has argued.

As to the details of the interpretation—our insistence on a double influencing or a double invasion of the lower Pasión, with the two events lasting from the beginning of the 10th Cycle until well after 10.3.0.0.0, and Thompson's lumping together of all of these things into a single invasion and a somewhat shorter overall span of time—there are differences between us and Thompson. They cannot yet be resolved to everyone's satisfaction. His reconstruction has the advantage of being the simpler; ours, I think, makes a better attempt at trying to incorporate a greater range of archaeological evidence. We can only hope that future investigations will result in improved or more satisfying reconstructions of these puzzling events of the ninth and tenth centuries.

For the present, though, it can be said that Thompson's approach to the role of the Chontal-Putun in these events through ethnohistoric sources and the relation of these to archaeology has done a great deal to expand our knowledge of the Classic Maya denouement; and it is not boastful to claim that our work at Altar de Sacrificios, and at Seibal, has also helped to open up this important line of investigation.

The causes of the Maya Classic decline and collapse are, to my way of thinking, directly involved with the alien pressures here identified as Chontal or Putun. Thompson does not think so, or at best, he would see these non-Classic Maya as only indirectly involved. He still favors a "proletarian" or peasant revolt as the explanation or the cause. It may well be that such popular unrest was a part of the chain of events that led to the desertion of the big southern lowland centers at the end of the ninth century, but I do not find this very satisfactory as a basic cause. Maya Classic civilization had flourished for a long time without such unrest. One is led to ask, Why the unrest? Why the revolt, at this particular time? To attribute it to sheer lower-class cussedness does not take us very far on the way to understanding. I would suggest, instead, that Maya Classic Period troubles, including all of the exacerbations of preexisting stresses and strains within that society, were most basically instigated by the cutting off of trade, to the west and to the north, and that this was done by the Chontal or Putun Maya. Some few sites, such as Seibal, were given a brief, late lease on life by Putun alliances; but, as the Postclassic Period continued, such sites were found to be too far from the coast and from the main trade routes to be maintained as profitable concerns.[33]

33. This follows the hypotheses advanced by Webb (1964, 1973) and Rathje (1971b, 1973). See also Willey and Shimkin (1971).

IV

TRENDS

THIS SECTION is intended as a diachronic viewing of the same data which we have already considered under the heading "Culture-Historical Integration" as a series of synchronic "cross sections" or culture phases. There the emphasis was on synchronic integration; here it is on culture change through time.[34]

I will attempt to make such a diachronic presentation on both the level of the factual data and on the level of behavioral or institutional inference drawn from these data—much as was done in the "Culture-Historical Integration" section. Again, the focus of attention is on the site of Altar de Sacrificios; but, again, I will take some cognizance of the larger setting of the Maya southern lowlands as a whole.

SETTLEMENT

The settlement (and architectural) trends at Altar de Sacrificios throughout the Preclassic and into the Protoclassic occupations are very definitely those of increasing growth and elaboration.

In Xe times we have evidence of small structure occupations under the Group B Plaza area and in the area to the west of Group B. The architecture of the phase is all quite simple—packed earth floor, pole constructions, wattle-and-daub walls, and thatched roofs. The reconstructed community picture is that of a small village on high ground near the Pasión-Salinas confluence. There are no good indications that any buildings were of a special size or elaboration to signify a temple, community building, or what we have come to think of in the Maya lowlands as a ceremonial center.

For the San Felix phase the general area of occupance is about the same as for Xe times—the Group B area plus the land immediately to the west; however, there was a small increase in the number of dwelling locations during the Xe phase. The more notable change, however, is in the presence of raised clay platforms for dwellings. Most houses had small platforms; and, toward the close of San Felix, some of these platforms in the Group B area are of a size (5 meters in height) and an elaboration (terraced and with *almeja* masonry coatings) to suggest that they were special buildings of a politico-religious significance.

The Plancha community at Altar is substantially larger than that of San Felix, in density of occupation if not in area. Many more dwelling locations are counted than in the previous phases. Also, by this time, the Group B takes on the unmistakable appearance of a ceremonial center. The tallest platform or mound, Structure B-I, has an imposing height of 9 meters in its final building stage. It also presents such features as multiple terraces, stairways of redstone, and basal molding and stucco design ornamentations. The ceremonial or politico-religious nature of the construction is further attested to by the presence of votive caches of pottery vessels placed in a building during its construction. The other three structures of B Group had also been enlarged and elaborated upon during this phase.

Overall settlement changes in the Salinas phase are slight. There is no increase in dwelling locations; in fact, there may be a slight drop-off. Growth, however, continues to be registered in the B Group ceremonial center with the Structure B-I pyramid being carried

34. Also on biological change through time, to a degree, as in one of the subsections to follow which deals with the Human Populations of Altar de Sacrificios.

still higher and faced with red sandstone block masonry. New architectural elaborative features are also added, and the placing of votive caches in the building continues.

The reasonable socio-political inferences that may be read into our Xe-through-Salinas trends at Altar de Sacrificios are those of community population increase with a changeover from simple village life to village-cum-ceremonial-center life under the leadership of an emerging elite. In drawing these inferences it must be noted that our settlement data are limited in a regional sense. Our detailed knowledge comes from the Altar center and its immediate environs. Beyond a kilometer or so from the site proper we have only a general knowledge of the existence of other small structure mounds (presumably dwelling locations) and lesser ceremonial centers along the lower Pasión; we do not know the dating of these mounds or centers and cannot offer any kind of a guess as to the size and nature of the lower Pasión Valley populations surrounding (and perhaps supporting) Altar de Sacrificios during these Preclassic-Protoclassic phases.

There are no significant architectural innovations or additions in the Group B ceremonial center in Early Classic times at Altar. This is the period of the Ayn and Verēmos phases, corresponding, we believe, to the northeast Peten Tzakol 2 and 3 phases. The principal changes in the center are the first appearances of carved and dated stelae in the Ayn phase, these dating between 9.1.0.0.0 and 9.4.10.0.0 (or A.D. 455–524). Dwelling site occupations decline in number from those counted for the Plancha and Salinas phases; however, these figures may be misleading in site population estimates in that the Ayn and Veremos phases, taken together, span a much shorter period of time than either the Plancha or Salinas phases. The Veremos phase falls somewhere within the Classic Maya stelae hiatus, at apparently a time of short-lived crisis in southern lowland Maya culture (Willey 1973) so the slackening in architectural activity, and perhaps even in site population, is in keeping with areawide trends for the latter decades of the Early Classic; but the general lack of large ceremonial construction at Altar in the earlier Ayn phase is out of developmental synchronization with the building that was going on in the northeast Peten at this time.

At some time after the close of the Ayn phase the ceremonial center activities at Altar de Sacrificios are shifted from the B Group area of the site to what was to become the larger A Group Plaza. The earliest sizable buildings of Group A date to the Chixoy phase. Chixoy, which marks the beginnings of the Late Classic, and which has a general ceramic correspondence to Tepeu 1, shows a slight increase in house mound occupations over Veremos, and there is also a resumption of the stelae cult after the hiatus.

The Pasión phase is the Late Classic ceremonial center climax for Altar de Sacrificios, corresponding chronologically, and in ceramic typology, to Tepeu 2 of the northeast Peten. At this time the Altar de Sacrificios architects and builders shift from red sandstone to limestone, and the big platforms forming the North Plaza of A Group, Structures A-I, A-II, and A-III, and the ball court, Structure A-V, are constructed and carried to their final, or near-final, form. A number of monuments, both stelae and altars, are dedicated in this plaza during the Pasión phase. These major construction and monumental activities are accompanied by an increase in dwelling locations.

The Boca phase, which is the Terminal Late Classic phase at Altar de Sacrificios, sees relatively little building although some additions and modifications are made on the A Group platforms. The site is, however, more densely settled at this time than at any point in its pre-Columbian history, with virtually all of the house mounds at the western edge of the site showing signs of occupance. The ceramic crossties of the Boca phase are essentially those of the Tepeu 3 sphere.

The Jimba phase, which is dated to the Early Postclassic Period, sees drastic changes. There is no ceremonial construction in Group A or elsewhere at the site. Instead, there are indications that A Group was used largely as a living space, probably with only pole-and-thatch buildings. Only a relatively few of the western area mound platforms were occupied at this time.

To sum up Classic and Postclassic settlement and architectural trends, we see, first of all, a noticeable difference in overall developmental pattern between what happened in these later periods in contrast to the Preclassic-Protoclassic. Whereas the earlier trends had been those of population growth and ceremonial center elaboration, the Early Classic Period begins with, at best, a stabilization of population and a decline or stoppage in large construction. It does enjoy, however, an inception of elaborate monumental carving in the appearance of the stelae cult in the Ayn phase. In the succeeding Veremos phase, however, there is a probable population fall, a continued lack of building activity, and a cessation of monumental activity. In this Veremos decline, which comes at the end of the Early Classic, Altar seems to have been either following the lead of events in other Maya lowland centers, such as those of the northeast Peten, or, at least, responding to the same forces that were affecting these other sites. This synchronization of the fortunes of Altar de Sacrificios with the northeast Peten continues on into the Late Classic, this time to its advantage, with the population boom and architectural and monumental florescence of the Pasión phase. The Terminal Late Classic Boca phase also parallels events in other southern lowland great centers, with a fading of architectural activity and of the stelae cult. However, there is a difference at Altar in that there would appear to be a continued population upswing at this point in time. Here, our controlled data bear only upon the immediate Altar de Sacrificios site, but our wider survey impressions suggest that this relatively heavy population may have characterized the whole lower Pasión region. The Jimba phase at Altar is unique and almost certainly indicative of an alien, Postclassic intrusion of non-Classic Maya peoples who did little more than camp on the old settlement area.

THE HUMAN POPULATIONS

On the matter of genetic continuity or discontinuity in the Altar populations we just do not know. The physical anthropological opinion is that all of the skeletal material seems to fall within expectable Mesoamerican-Maya bounds, but this leaves matters in very broad definition. In brief, the data are such that they do not preclude new population increments at various times during the sequence—nor, on the other hand, do they demonstrate them. This is unfortunate as there are at least three places in the Altar sequence where the cultural evidence could be interpreted as indicative of alien population invasion, with partial or even full replacement. In my own opinion, which already has been expressed on this point, I do not think that there was any significant new population increment at Altar de Sacrificios until the close of the Boca phase, at which time I believe there was a massive incremental addition or, possibly, a complete replacement; however, this opinion derives entirely from an appraisal of cultural data.

The small size of the human skeletal series for some of the Altar de Sacrificios phases makes trend plotting difficult or hazardous. One of the few clear time trends is in stature. The Preclassic male Altarians were taller than those of the Classic-Early Postclassic; and all of these averaged taller than present-day Maya lowland males. The female Altarians do not show any pre-Columbian trend in this regard although, as a whole, they were taller than present-day Maya lowland women.

Bone pathologies were very common among ancient Altarians. For the earliest phase, the Xe, we have only one human skeleton, a male. This was a robust young adult with no significant pathology; but following this, all other Preclassic and Classic-Early Postclassic phases showed considerable pathology. As early as San Felix we note cranial osteitis (probably indicative of syphilis or yaws), subperiosteal hemorrhaging evidences and periodontal degeneration (both suggestive of vitamin deficiencies), enamel hypoplasia of the teeth (a sign of childhood nutritional problems or disease), spongy-porotic hypertosis (indicative of anemia, possibly from chronic childhood diarrhea), and dental caries. All of these conditions appear to persist from San Felix through Jimba. In addition, arthritic conditions of the bone are definite as early as the Ayn phase and continue thereafter. One very important factor in disease and health conditions at Altar de Sacrificios would appear to have been nutritional deficiencies; however, we can plot no trend of worsening, or bettering, in this.

Cultural modifications were made in the human body in some of the Altar phases, and there are some chronological differentiations or trends in these. The filing of the teeth (incisors) of adults began as early as the Plancha phase and continued from this time through the Jimba phase. Dental inlays (of jadeites or pyrites) were not this early. From our evidence, they occur only in the Pasión phase. Cranial deformation was probably only a Late Classic-Early Postclassic trait at Altar. There are a couple of earlier instances of possibly deformed skulls, one as early as the Salinas phase; but the very clear-cut, obviously artificial, fronto-occipital deformation, of the tabular-oblique and tabular-erect varieties, does not appear until Pasión. It is then recorded in the subsequent Boca and Jimba phases. Both males and females had been so treated.

MONUMENTAL ART, INSCRIPTIONS, CALENDRICS

Monumental stone art, hieroglyphic inscriptions, and Maya calendrics and mathematics are three closely related subsystems in Classic lowland Maya culture. How early do they appear, what are their origins, and what is their developmental history during the Classic Period? At Altar de Sacrificios the answers, or tentative answers, to all of these questions are much the same as they are at other Peten Maya sites. In the Middle Preclassic Xe phase (ca. 900–600 B.C.) there are no clues to any of these things. In fact, there is no good evidence of a ceremonial center, or clustering of non-dwelling, politico-religious buildings, where such carved monuments usually occur, in that phase. Nor are there any signs of monumental art, inscriptions, or calendrics in the succeeding San Felix (ca. 600–300 B.C.) when a small, but probable, ceremonial center comes into existence. Even in the Plancha phase (ca. 300 B.C.–A.D. 150), with its large, terraced, and *almeja* masonry-covered pyramid, there is very little that could be designated as monumental art. A stucco scroll element, found on the floor of one of the upper terraces of the Structure B-I pyramid, would probably qualify, but there is little else. It is not until the Salinas phase, dated at A.D. 150–450, that we have the first Altar de Sacrificios carved monuments. Even at this time there is some doubt about such an early placement of the carved Censer Altar C, although its dragonlike carving is very similar to Late Preclassic or Protoclassic masks at Uaxactun and, somewhat more remotely, is suggestive of Late Preclassic Kaminaljuyu art. With the beginning of the Ayn phase we have the first Initial Series stela at Altar de Sacrificios, a monument dating at 9.1.0.0.0 (A.D. 455).

The source of inspiration—and probably instruction—for these earliest monuments and inscriptions at Altar de Sacrificios was almost certainly the northeast Peten where Initial Series stelae date back to the latter part of Cycle 8; however, it is well to keep in mind that the Preclassic Altarians were probably generally familiar with hieroglyphics and calendrical systems. We have mentioned the El Porton monuments of the Baja Verapaz, with their glyphs and numbers. These may have been as early as Xe or San Felix; at the latest they were contemporaneous with Plancha. It is quite likely that the El Porton peoples were of Maya speech; in fact, they may have been of a stock ancestral to the early Xe settlers of the Peten. So a sharing of knowledge and a tradition of a calendar and writing, between Preclassic highlander and lowlander does not seem out of the question even though the lowlanders may not yet have been familiar enough with this kind of learning to carve and erect monuments memorializing it. Apparently, the first successful lowland attempts along this line were those of the northeast Peten, from whence the stelae cult spread to other parts of the lowlands. The readiness with which the cult was accepted in other places, such as at Altar de Sacrificios, suggests some foreknowledge of the ideas involved.

During the Early Classic Ayn phase there

were at least five Initial Series stelae set up at Altar de Sacrificios, all in B Group ceremonial plaza. They date from 9.1.0.0.0 to 9.4.10.0.0 (A.D. 455–524). In addition, a number of other monuments (plain stelae, altars) fall somewhere in the Early Classic Period time range of the Ayn-Veremos phases. It is of interest to observe the internal development of the Group B early stelae. The earliest of the five are purely glyphic, with no portraits of individuals, but the latest two have such portraits in addition to their texts. There is also a steady increase through time in the numbers of glyphs that occur on these five monuments. The earlier ones have relatively few glyphs, in addition to the Initial Series date and the lunar series; the later ones show more texts that are apparently noncalendrical. In view of their association with the portraits it is not unreasonable to think that these noncalendrical texts may have pertained to historical and dynastic matters. This trend in stelae and glyphic text development is not unique to Altar de Sacrificios but is seen throughout the southern lowlands in the Early Classic, and it becomes especially pronounced as the sequence of monuments progresses from the Early Classic to the Late Classic. Thus, we are dealing with the diffusion of a highly complex cultural subsystem, closely interrelated from site to site. At the same time, these changes in the hieroglyphic, monumental, artistic, and calendrical subsystems must have been closely interrelated to developments in other aspects of culture—developments taking place in the Altar de Sacrificios community as well as elsewhere which were leading toward the formation of an increasingly nonegalitarian, hierarchically structured Maya society.

The temporary cessation of stelae erection at Altar de Sacrificios at shortly after 9.4.10.0.0 (A.D. 524), with perhaps only a few plain monuments set up in the decades immediately thereafter, corresponds to what has been referred to as the Classic Maya "hiatus." This cessation, or near-cessation, of stelae carving and erection throughout the southern lowlands has been noted by various authors writing on the Maya, and recently I have devoted a brief paper to the subject (Willey 1973). In this paper I express the opinion that the hiatus in stelae dedication, which occurs between 9.5.0.0.0 and 9.8.0.0.0 (A.D. 534–593), is truly reflective of a pause or a faltering in Classic Maya high ceremonial activities which signals a crisis of some sort afflicting the southern lowland Maya leadership at that time. I advance the hypothesis that the historical, and the functional, cause of this crisis was the withdrawal of Teotihuacan-directed trade and symbiotic support that had been an important element in Maya lowland ceremonial-center growth in the preceding centuries of the Early Classic Period. This thesis and its development are relatively complex, and we will not go into them at any great length here; however, the hiatus in stelae erection does concern us in our examination of change and trends in the monumental art-hieroglyphic-calendric activities at Altar de Sacrificios, and it deserves some further comment. In discussing the matter with me, the epigrapher of the Altar de Sacrificios monuments, John A. Graham, revealed a somewhat different set of views, and I would like to present these here, in a long quotation from a letter to me in September 1972. Graham writes:

> The Altar de Sacrificios monuments contribute a certain amount of important light upon the socalled "hiatus," the period from about 9.5.0.0.0 to 9.8.0.0.0 in which few stelae are known and which is therefore characterized by a number of students as a "general cessation of stela erections." At Altar the stela gap is particularly evident, separating the Early Classic stelae of Group B and the Late Classic monuments of the South Plaza of Group A. At Temple B-I the latest surviving monument is Stela 12, marking 9.4.10.0.0, although there is a gap in the balanced arrangement of monuments there suggesting that a monument was planned for the 9.5.0.0.0 ending. In Group A's South Plaza the stela record next takes up with Stela 18/B, bearing the inscribed date of 9.9.5.0.0. The front of this monument (designated Stela 18/F) had originally been carved with a portrait and the Initial Series date of 9.4.0.0.0 and was almost surely erected at that date at Temple B-I. Its removal to the South Plaza to be reerected with a hieroglyphic text and Initial Series date of 9.9.5.0.0 added to its previously uncarved back thus appears to mark the end of the Altar hiatus. Since the original 9.4.0.0.0 portrait and text of the front of the stela were not altered, it suggested that the rulers of the day sought identifica-

tion with earlier authority and, to a certain extent, were reiterating the old orthodoxy. Could we read the lengthy text accompanying the 9.9.5.0.0 Initial Series on the back of the monument we would probably have valuable clues to the nature of the preceding hiatus.

The argument that there was a general cessation of stela carving during the hiatus does not seem entirely attractive upon the evidence of the next stelae to be raised at Altar de Sacrificios: Stela 8, at 9.9.15.0.0, and Stela 9, at 9.10.0.0.0, ten and fifteen years later, respectively. The portraits of both of these monuments, though very poorly preserved, exhibit striking advances in the stela art when compared to the portraits of Stela 18/F at 9.4.0.0.0 and Stela 12 at 9.4.10.0.0, immediately prior to the hiatus. The solution offered to old problems and the development of new approaches point to considerable sculptural activity during the hiatus. Clearly, there is no mere picking up where the artists of Stela 12 and 18/F left off. At Altar de Sacrificios, therefore, the question becomes: Does the local hiatus reflect a true cessation of monument carving which came to an end with the reinstitution of orthodoxy and the importation of Late Classic Maya art from other centers where sculpture must have continued to be carved during the hiatus, or were hiatus stelae carved at Altar only to be subjected to a thorough destruction (as presumably occurred at many other sites)? Since demolished stelae may have been dumped at some distance away from the ceremonial center, or buried deeply in structural fill, our failure to find fragments that could be attributed to the hiatus cannot be considered acceptable negative evidence, and the question must remain open.

Graham's argument, that Late Classic Maya stelae after the hiatus show a considerable artistic evolution beyond those of immediately pre-hiatus time, is a significant one; and we must suspect that stylistic development in monumental art, as well as hieroglyphic and calendrical scholarship had not stood still for the 60 years or so of the hiatus. Just how the gap was bridged remains a mystery. We know of a few 9.6.0.0.0 and 9.7.0.0.0 monuments at some Maya sites, principally sites on the far western, eastern, and northern borders of the southern lowlands. Perhaps the crisis of the sixth century A.D., if such it was, did not affect the peripheries in the same way that it did the Peten heartland, and developments in these provincial sites carried on the traditions of orthodoxy (to use Graham's term) and passed them back to the old original centers. Or, perhaps, as Graham has suggested, stelae of the hiatus interval were, for some reason, mutilated, smashed, or hidden—at Altar de Sacrificios and elsewhere. The question is, indeed, open; but I like the former explanation better, for I find it hard to believe that such iconoclasm would have been directed only at those monuments of the hiatus interval and not at the earlier ones which were left remaining and in full view in the ceremonial precinct of the site.

After the hiatus there were three Initial Series stelae set up at Altar de Sacrificios in either the brief Chixoy phase or in the early part of the succeeding Pasión phase. These were Stela 18/B, the reworked earlier monument referred to by Graham in his letter, and Stelae 8 and 9. The dedicatory dates are 9.9.5.0.0, 9.9.15.0.0, and 9.10.0.0.0, spanning from A.D. 618 to 633. All were in the South Plaza of A Group, and all were of red sandstone in the manner of the Early Classic monuments. It is also likely that at about this same time some red sandstone altars were also carved and placed in the North Plaza of A Group. Shortly after 9.10.0.0.0 there was a switch from red sandstone to limestone—a switch noted also in architectural as well as monument material—and Stelae 4 and 5, dedicated at 9.10.10.0.0 (A.D. 642) and 9.11.0.0.0. (A.D. 652) mark this changeover. Both monuments were located in the North Plaza of Group A, and both were wall panels rather than true stelae, although they bear Initial Series dates. Other sculptured panels and a number of true stelae were placed in the North Plaza over the next several decades, with the last Initial Series dedication date at 9.17.0.0.0 (A.D. 771) or almost at the close of the Pasión phase. These Pasión phase monuments mark the climax of the stela cult at Altar de Sacrificios. They relate closely to other southern lowland stelae and altars of the Late Classic; and Graham summarizes them by saying that they have chronological statements, lunar texts, the Uniform base used in moon counting, and many names of individuals and titles.

Only a single monument is attributed to the Boca phase. This is a stelae with a Giant Ahau rather than an Initial Series date. Graham has placed it at 10.1.0.0.0 (A.D. 849), or well into the time of the decline of the stela cult throughout the southern lowlands.

The Jimba phase has no monuments.

The occurrence patterns and the trends in monumental arts, hieroglyphs, and calendrics at Altar de Sacrificios can be summed up by saying that the earliest Initial Series monuments appear at the beginning of Cycle 9, with the probability of some monumental art (Censer Altar C) being a little earlier than this. These early Cycle 9 stelae, which are very similar to those of the northeast Peten, show a steady increase in the numbers of non-calendric glyphs, and this, taken together with the appearance of portraits of individuals on the later ones, suggests an increasing concern with political and probably lineage matters. After a hiatus, corresponding roughly to the general southern lowland stelae hiatus of the latter part of the sixth century A.D., monumental art and glyphic texts reappear at Altar in a pattern of Late Classic florescence in the seventh and eighth centuries. While concerned with chronology and astronomical matters, as usual, these Late Classic stelae at Altar de Sacrificios follow general Late Classic trends in treating what would appear to be the political concerns and the names of personages and titles.

In the ninth century there is a very definite decline in stelae carving and erection at Altar which corresponds to the areawide Late Classic decline. The last monument at Altar de Sacrificios dates at A.D. 849.

CRAFT GOODS

Altar de Sacrificios ceramics of the Xe phase are in an early southern Mesoamerican tradition of competently made but rather simple vessel forms (including the shallow plate, tecomate, and necked jar), monochrome surfacing (in red, black, and cream-white), and modest incised-punctated decoration. Although the origin point of this tradition, as far as the lower Pasión Valley is concerned, is not surely known, there are clues which point to the Guatemalan highlands and particularly the Alta Verapaz and the Baja Verapaz. Once in the southern lowlands, this early southern Mesoamerican ceramic tradition tends to become progressively more standardized, in vessel forms and polished monochrome surface finishings. Although truly elaborate wares are never a part of this southern Maya lowland Preclassic pottery development, it is probably fair to say that there is a slight but steady trend toward "elegance." Toward the end of the Plancha phase (Chicanel sphere) the Altar ceramics begin to respond to outside influences from more sophisticated pottery-making centers—centers which probably lie outside the southern Maya lowlands. This is seen in the apparent local manufacture of pottery with painted decoration imitating upland Usulutan ware and banded appliqué styles.

The real separation between what might be thought of as unslipped and monochrome cooking, water-storage, and household wares, on the one hand, and fine quality household, ritual, or burial pottery, on the other, does not begin until the Protoclassic Salinas phase when we see the first fine wares in true Usulutan pottery (whether made locally or imported is undetermined) and in locally produced positive-painted polychromes, such as the Ixcanrio type. The latter begins the orange background with red and black decoration that is to characterize Maya Classic polychrome for the next several hundred years. Polychrome painting is a firm part of the Maya pottery tradition by the succeeding Ayn phase (Tzakol sphere). Another important ceramic element of Ayn is the tripod cylinder jar, a vessel form quite obviously inspired by Teotihuacan influences. The Veremos phase marks a transition in the Classic polychromes from the Tzakol to the Tepeu horizon while the Chixoy and Pasión phases see the full development of these Tepeu sphere polychromes at Altar. In the Pasión phase a local regional trend sets in, particularly in monochromes and coarser wares; however, there is still a common southern lowland sharing in polychrome, figure-painted cylinder jars, and, indeed, some of the finest specimens at Altar may have been made in other centers and brought to, or traded into, the site as funerary ware for the elite class. In the succeeding Boca phase the regional separatism of Altar de Sacrificios common pottery is even more marked. There is also now a decline in polychrome pottery, and the few polychrome types that do occur show a reduction in the elaborateness of painted design. Toward the close of the Boca phase Fine Orange and Fine Gray wares of a radically different pottery tradition from that of the Classic Maya make their appearance, presumably as trade into the lower Pasión region from the Gulf coast-lower Usumacinta country.

The ceramics of the Jimba phase are entirely in this new Fine Orange-Fine Gray tradition. This applies to both everyday wares and to finer decorated pieces. In other words, in this final phase at Altar there has been an almost total replacement of the old resident Classic Maya ceramic complex.

The trends and patterns through time of the pottery figurine-making at Altar de Sacrificios can be summed up quite simply. The Xe-San Felix figurines are, like the ceramics of those phases, in a general southern Mesoamerican Preclassic tradition. There are close resemblances to figurines of the Guatemalan highlands. These are solid, handmade figurines, usually in the female form. By the Late Preclassic Plancha phase they have largely disappeared. Thereafter, there are no figurines in the Altar sequence until Late Classic times when they probably begin in the Chixoy phase and reach florescence in the succeeding Pasión and Boca phases. They also continue in the Jimba phase. Most of them are hollow figurine-whistles. Virtually all are moldmade. Many are very Classic Maya-like, with men and priest-figures resembling the figures of monumental Classic sculptures; however, some, made of Fine Orange or Fine Gray paste, and dating from the Jimba phase, are in a non-Classic Maya style and portray individuals who seem alien to the Classic Maya context.

In considering figurines, it should be made clear that the Middle Preclassic handmade figures and those of the hollow moldmade types are in quite different traditions. There is a definite discontinuity between them—at Altar de Sacrificios and in other lowland Maya sites. They may have served quite different functions.

Perforated disk spindle whorls were used throughout most of the Altar sequence, but in the Terminal Late Classic moldmade whorls partially replaced them. Of the few other trends or occurrence patterns to be noted in miscellaneous ceramic manufactures we can cite: 1) pottery stamps as being more typical of the Preclassic; and 2) pottery ear ornaments beginning as early as Plancha but having their greatest variety and elaboration in Pasión.

In ground stone utility implements the basin-shaped or turtlebacked metate is found throughout the sequence and was, obviously, the most important maize-grinding implement; however, in the Late Classic a new type, a thin flat metate appears. Some of these had small tripod legs and a peculiar surface grooving. These last appear too small and too delicate for maize-grinding. Mano stones occur throughout the sequence, and the only notable change in these is that beginning with the Pasión phase the majority of them are standardized to a square cross section variety. Ring-stones or doughnut stones appear for the first time in the Pasión phase and are found in numbers thereafter. Their function is unknown. Barkbeaters, while probably occurring earlier, are mostly a Late Classic item. Small polished stone celts are found intermittently throughout the sequence; presumably there was a continuity in these, but they were relatively rare.

Small ornamental ground stones—pendants and beads—occur as early as San Felix and Plancha; however, jadeite beads and the use of jadeite polished flakes in the making of mosaic items peak in the Classic Period, but with a decline in Boca.

The chipped flint celt or land-clearing implement is the common chipped stone form throughout the Altar sequence and the only even moderately specialized form in the Preclassic. At some time in the Protoclassic-to-Early Classic laurel-leaf blades and flint eccentrics appear. These presumably ceremonial forms last for some time, but they begin to be quite rare in the Boca phase. By Jimba times they are gone. Large tapered-stem spearpoints come in for the first time in Chixoy; and they continue in numbers through Pasión, Boca, and, possibly, Jimba. Toward the end of the sequence a few straight-stemmed and fishtail points also make an appearance.

Obsidian prismatic bladelets appear throughout the sequence but are more numerous in Classic times. From Chixoy and Pasión we have a few laurel-leafs and eccentrics in this material, and from Chixoy times on there are also a few stemmed obsidian points, similar in form to the flint ones.

The first artifacts made from marine shells come into the sequence in Plancha times, and more occur during the Classic phases, climaxing in Pasión. Stingray spines, a definite ritual item, as well as a marine product, are also found from Ayn through Pasión. In Boca and Jimba there are few such shells and no stingray spines. In other words, the pattern suggests the greatest coastal trade contacts in the Early Classic and the first two centuries of the Late Classic, with a cutoff or drop-off afterward.

TREATMENT OF THE DEAD

There is a definite time trend in the Altar de Sacrificios burial sequence for more differentiation—in the nature of the grave, in the place of the grave, and in the amount and elaborateness of grave goods—among individuals interred; that is, the ready inference may be drawn of more "democratic" earlier practices versus more "aristocratic" later practices. This trend continues, with some irregularity at about the time of the hiatus, to peak in the Pasión phase. There is some drop-off, away from the elaboration of the burials of the most distinguished dead in the Boca phase and a complete reduction of differentiation and elaboration in the Jimba phase. The record may be recounted in somewhat more detail as follows.

Xe and San Felix burials were all simple pit interments, made in or near dwellings. The single Xe burial had no accompanying grave goods. All of those identified with the San Felix phase had at least one pot; and, in addition, a small stone pendant and a polished celt were found, respectively, with two others.

With the Plancha phase we have the first burials which are placed in crypt and stone cist graves. Such graves were made in ceremonial center or politico-religious buildings. Pottery vessels were found with most Plancha burials; and jadeite beads and other small ornaments also occur with some.

For Salinas, while we have no cist or crypt graves, there is an increase in grave goods found with some burials, with shell and pyrite composite adornos, stingray spines, and more jadeite beads. The Ayn phase pattern is much the same but with an increase in the amounts of exotic objects occurring with some burials.

Veremos and Chixoy burials are relatively few in number. The ones recorded are all simple in grave form, and the burial accompaniments are mostly ceramic.

With Pasión there is an upswing in elaboration again, with both cist and crypt graves (one of each) and with some burials, such as the lady in Burial 128, surrounded with pottery vessels and adorned with jadeites, shell items, stingray spines, and other small goods.

Boca shows a decline from these standards of elaboration and wealth, and with the simple Jimba phase burials we found little except pottery and sometimes not even that.

For further and exact correlations of burial forms, place of interment, grave goods, such things as dental inlays and filing and cranial flattening, and age and sex data of individuals—all arranged by phase—the reader should see Smith (1972, table 5).

One comparative observation is also worth recording here. I am indebted to my colleague William A. Haviland who writes (2 October 1970) as follows:

> Something which may interest you, as it did me when I discovered it this summer; we don't know the real sex ratio for Tikal, for the bone sample is biased in favor of males by our concentration on structures, as opposed to plazas and other areas. Apparently, structures were favored places for burials, and males were more often so-buried than females. The sex ratio of 220 for Tikal reflects this bias, rather than the real proportion of males to females. I am fascinated, then, to find that Frank Saul's data for Altar suggest a ratio of 152 for that site. Granting an emphasis there on structures vs. non-structures, I wonder if this isn't one more indication of status differences vis-à-vis the sexes between the two sites?

With regard to this, we call attention to the female burials, Nos. 128 and 96, of the Pasión phase, which were buried, respectively, in a crypt and a cist grave, both accompanied with numerous and rich grave objects. Females were buried in the Altar ceremonial center as early as San Felix times; however, their proportions increase in the Late Classic phases.

VOTIVE CACHES

The earliest Altar de Sacrificios votive caches are those of the Late Preclassic Plancha phase. These caches consisted always of pottery vessels, usually placed in ceremonial-center structures. In some few instances these vessels contained such items as obsidian bladelets and jadeite beads. Caches of pottery vessels were also found in Salinas structures, especially the multicache, or huge cache, deposit discovered under the main stairway of the Structure B-I temple pyramid. Some other cached vessels identified with the phase contained such things as stingray spines and fishbones. It is also possible—although the dating is not entirely secure—that caches of 9 and 13 objects (flint eccentrics or obsidians) taken from under altars belong to the Salinas phase. By Ayn times the practice of caching flints (including eccentrics), obsidians, and other small objects under altars or stelae seems to have been established. This, of course, is a common and widespread Maya lowland pattern.

At Altar de Sacrificios we found few such caches that could be securely related to the brief Veremos and Chixoy phases, but a number of them date to the Pasión phase. In Boca times these were more rare, a circumstance probably correlated with the decline of stelae and altar dedication in this phase; however, pottery vessel caches and some caches of obsidians and flint flakes are recorded. A few pottery caches are also identified with the Jimba phase.

V

CLOSING COMMENT ON INITIAL PROBLEMS

A PROPER concluding statement to a work such as this should refer back to the problems which were conceived at the outset as guides to research and attempt to appraise just how far we have gone toward their solution. This section is intended as that. The problems, as we saw them at the beginning of the Altar de Sacrificios investigations in 1958 and 1959, may be summarized as follows:

1. The need for basic formal-spatial-temporal data on the southwestern Peten or lower Pasión region
   a. Ceramic
   b. Artifactual
   c. Architectural
   d. Monumental, hieroglyphic, calendric
   e. Settlement
2. More information on Maya highland-lowland relationships
   a. Preclassic origins
   b. Late relationships
3. Altar de Sacrificios as a "crossroads"
   a. The interrelating of lowland regional sequences
   b. An investigation of Altar as a trading center (a problem afterthought)
4. Mexican relationships to the lowland Maya
   a. On a Teotihuacan or Early Classic horizon
   b. On a later horizon
5. Questions of functional (and processual) implications
   a. Particularly as might be elucidated through settlement data

Now, at the close of our work, how much have we done? What remains to be done?

On the first score, that of basic data gathering, we have made a sound beginning. A basic sequence carried out largely in ceramics, has been established for Altar de Sacrificios. This sequence runs from the Middle Preclassic to the Early Postclassic. The sequence is well crosstied to other southern lowland sequences. Within the site itself ceramic chronology is reasonably well coordinated with other aspects of culture—although on this last point, as has been indicated, there are still some questions and doubts. A large number of artifacts have been examined and reasonably well dated within the sequence frame of reference. Architectural forms have been explored with considerable thoroughness, and these have been dated, relatively through pottery and, in some cases, absolutely through Initial Series stelae dates. They have also been compared and contrasted to architectural forms in other Maya lowland regions. Monuments, hieroglyphics, and calendrics have been studied in good detail. Those known from earlier explorations (especially Morley) have been reexamined, and, in some instances new interpretations and datings have been advanced. Several new monuments were also discovered. The immediate Altar de Sacrificios settlement (adjoining the ceremonial center) has been mapped and virtually all of the structures within it have been test excavated.

On the matter of highland-lowland relationships we have some clues but no great amount of new information. There is, indeed, some disagreement between Adams and myself over the origins of our earliest Middle Preclassic phase, the Xe. I am more ready to accept a Guatemalan highland origin than is Adams, who would prefer to keep open a number of other possibilities (El Salvador, the northern lowlands, the southern Mexican Gulf coast). There are, of course, several Classic Period highland ceramic ties to Altar as has been pointed out by Adams.

It is still difficult to appraise the "crossroads" functions of Altar de Sacrificios. Was it a very important trading post and also a strategic military location at the confluence of the major rivers on which it was located? The best we can say is, probably. The ceramic sequence of the site certainly reflects cross-currents of influence. This sequence relates very closely to the east and the north in its Preclassic and much of its Classic Period development. There are also differences between Altar and the northeast Peten sequences. For example, some Protoclassic elements, such as Usulutan ware, are much more common at Altar than in the north and east: and in the Terminal Late Classic Period Altar comes increasingly under the influence of a lower Usumacinta-Gulf coast ceramic tradition of Fine Orange and Fine Gray wares.

The nature of these influences has not been fully determined in all cases. The Fine Orange and Fine Gray wares at Altar are undoubtedly trade pieces, made somewhere in the lower Usumacinta-Gulf coast region and brought to Altar. Some Late Classic polychromes which we found were also probably made elsewhere and imported to Altar as luxury goods, and the same is probably also true of the Protoclassic Period Usulutan ware; however, much more investigation is needed on regional identifications of ceramic manufactures, through neutron activation and other kinds of analyses, before we can speak with assurance about Maya lowland ceramic trade. We know that the Altarians engaged in ceramic trade to an extent, but whether they were more active in this regard than the inhabitants of other Maya lowland centers has not been demonstrated. With reference to other commodities of trade, the Altar handling of such things as obsidian, jadeite, or marine shells does not seem to have been on a large scale. Obsidian bladelets are abundant there but probably no more than in other Peten sites of comparable size; and there were no large fat cores of obsidian of the kind that one might expect would have been stored at a great trading post for this resource. Jadeite was present, both in the raw state and in small ornaments, but the quantities could not be called abundant. Quite possibly, Altar served as a redistribution point for salt which was brought down the Salinas from deposits in the highlands, but we have no proof of this—at least that we could recognize.

As to Mexican relationships, Altar's Teotihuacan influences are noticeable but not massive. We found some fine pottery vessels with some Early Classic burials that were made in a Teotihuacan manner; but these would appear to be Mayan manufactures, either local or from some nearby regions, rather than actual Mexican imports. In general, the Teotihuacanoid impress at Altar de Sacrificios is much less than it is at Tikal which is much farther to the east and north. That is, Altar's more westerly geographical position does not seem to be correlated with increased Teotihuacanoid influences. On the other hand, Altar's later Mexicanoid influences are considerable; and, as we have said, this was one of the surprises of the excavations. We have the evidence of the trade in fine paste wares and figurines in the latter part of the Boca phase and then the inundation of these wares and artifacts that marks the Early Postclassic Jimba phase, for which time we hypothesize an actual invasion by alien or non-Classic Maya peoples whose culture has a strong Toltecoid or Mexicanoid cast.

Finally, on questions of functional and processual implication, and especially with reference to the gathering and interpretation of settlement data, our efforts were very limited. We were unable to survey in detail beyond the limits of the terrain immediately adjacent to the Altar de Sacrificios ceremonial center so that our knowledge of the lower Pasión region as a whole remains very sketchy and general. However, with the settlement data which we did collect, taken in conjunction with our excavation data from the center, we have a basis for suggesting some hypotheses about social and cultural development at the site and for making a beginning in the testing of these hypotheses. And it is with these matters that we now wish to conclude.

VI

TOWARD PROCESS

THE SYNCHRONIC phase presentations and the diachronic tracing of trends do not constitute an analysis of culture process, but they are attempts to order and arrange the data as a preliminary to this. At this point, I would like to offer a tentative analysis of a limited selection of our data that, I hope, will point in the direction of processual understanding. For the time being, I shall go no further than this. There are various reasons for this hesitancy. For one thing, the Altar de Sacrificios investigations were planned and begun in 1958. The original motivating problems for the research were essentially descriptive-historical, the gathering of data and the determination of relationships among bodies of data as these are expressed in formal or typological resemblances. They were not formulated as sharply defined hypotheses with equally specific strategies designed for their testing. But, in addition to this, I also feel somewhat inhibited about a direct attack on questions of process, because, in spite of opinions to the contrary (Binford 1968), I am not convinced that the framing of hypotheses about the Maya lowland past can be done effectively and intelligently prior to a very substantial descriptive-historical amassment of the data.

I think that the furthest I would want to give ground in this particular argument is that hypothesis formulation and data collecting on the lower Pasión must be advanced together in an exploratory way, feeding into and correcting each other. While it is true that the data by themselves will never give us the answers to the most interesting and revealing questions about the past, I doubt if these questions can be properly put if we must draw largely upon a cultural-behavioral background of nineteenth and twentieth century western Europe and America in framing our hypotheses. To put it another way, I am unconvinced that archaeologists as yet have at their disposal a body of cross-cultural information which will allow them to make other than the most general correlations between material remains and socio-cultural institutions. Such a body of information is sorely needed, and I am optimistic that some day we will have it; but this will come about only through the detailed examinations and comparisons of many specific historical situations, of which the Maya lowland continuum is one. Until then, I would rather take things more slowly; however, my inhibitions and hesitations should not deter others who may wish to venture ahead more boldly with any of the data here which they may find fit to their purposes. Contrary to some of my colleagues, I do not find error or false starts (if such they may be) in honest research in any way "dangerous" to the future of archaeology in general or Maya studies in particular.

But to return to my exploratory analysis, let us ask, as we view the cultural trends at Altar de Sacrificios through time, what concatenations in the patterning of these trends, what covariances strike us as most obvious? There are, I think, several, but at this point it might make for a more approved and explicit treatment if we turned our approach around and looked at the data deductively. It is a generally held assumption that pre-Columbian lowland Maya society developed through time from an essentially village egalitarian condition to a village-cum-ceremonial center non-egalitarian one. A cursory review of the Maya site monographic literature available would appear to bear this out; but a number of interesting questions remain. Just how did this transformation take place? What changes may have set other changes in motion in a positive or reinforcing feedback manner? To what extent were these developments *in situ* in each Maya center or in the Maya lowlands at large? To what extent were they dependent upon external stimuli? Let us begin with the hypothesis that this change from an egalitarian to a nonegalitarian society occurred at Altar de Sacrificios and look for test data in the archaeological record to verify or disprove this hypothesis.

First, there are the sheerly demographic dimensions to this question. We know, from the general comparative analogical data that are available to us on human societies from many times and places, that substantial population numbers are a usual characteristic of nonegalitarian societies; and where there is time sequence information, the evolution from egalitarian to nonegalitarian is almost always accompanied by population increase. At Altar de Sacrificios the Middle Preclassic Xe phase is represented by a small villagelike cluster of dwellings, and there is only a very slight increase in the number of these dwellings, and by inference in population, in the succeeding San Felix phase. But from San Felix to the Late Preclassic Plancha phase there is a dramatic rise in dwelling locations and, presumably, population concentration. Unfortunately, we lack a larger regional settlement control on this increase which would enable us to say, with certainty, that we are dealing with an overall regional demographic increase. That is, it is just possible that there were no more people in the lower Pasión Valley region in Plancha times than in San Felix times and that the phenomenon which we observe at Altar de Sacrificios was nothing more than a settlement rearrangement with a concentrating of formerly dispersed peoples at a single site. However, such an interpretation is belied by our knowledge of the Maya lowlands as a whole, where settlement data from other sites and regions do indicate a genuine population upsurge at this same point in time.[35] On balance, then, this first, demographic test of an egalitarian-to-nonegalitarian societal status supports our hypothesis. Population at Altar de Sacrificios increased significantly from Middle Preclassic to Late Preclassic times.

As a second expectation in a dynamic situation of a developing complex society, we might anticipate architectural efforts over and above those of ordinary dwelling construction. The Xe phase shows nothing like this, and during the earlier part of the San Felix phase there is very little that could be so construed. But toward the close of San Felix some sizable earth platforms were built which strongly suggest corporate effort on the part of the local populations. With the Plancha phase such building efforts must have increased severalfold. A number of large and elaborate platform constructions were put up in the B Group complex of the site, climaxing in the Late Plancha B-I pyramid which was 10 meters high, masonry-faced, approached by stairs, terraced, and ornamented with basal moldings and stucco decorations. It is difficult to interpret such a building sequence as this as other than steadily increasing group effort and preoccupation with community or politico-religious architecture, carried out under centralized planning and direction. Thus, the architectural expectations of an egalitarian to a nonegalitarian social evolution are also well met in the Altar de Sacrificios data.

A concurrent trend is also seen in differential treatment of the dead. There are no signs of differential treatment of individuals in Xe or San Felix; but in the Plancha phase we have the earliest crypt and stone cist burial chambers, with these placed in the central community or politico-religious structures.

Other expectations in an egalitarian-to-nonegalitarian sequence would be the appearance of monumental art and other signs of high ritual life as well as luxury craft goods and exotic trade items. These are all missing from Xe and San Felix levels. In Plancha contexts they begin to be represented, although only faintly, with the first signs of luxury ceramics and jadeite ornaments with some burials. However, elaborations along this line were to follow immediately afterward in the Salinas (Protoclassic) and Ayn (Early Classic) phases, with fine polychrome pottery and exotics in the form of jadeite and marine shell jewelry. In the Ayn phase the first carved stelae appear.

We have in these data, I think, the elements of a processual development of a society. Agricultural villagers, quite probably from the Guatemalan highlands, first settled in the

35. For confirmation of this see Willey and Shimkin (1973) and the several articles in this same volume Culbert, ed. 1973).

Peten rain forests, on the lower Pasión River, in the Middle Preclassic Period. The culture that they brought with them, or that they were able to establish there in this "frontier" situation, was not as elaborate as that of their highland heritage which, at that time, probably had already passed over the egalitarian-to-nonegalitarian threshold. For a considerable period this lowland society remained on a simple organizational level. From the sequence record of events that is available to us it would appear that changes in the cultural system began with a population increase which, in turn, seems likely to have been linked to agricultural or subsistence success. This success possibly may have been due to plant innovations or new cultivation techniques although we have no evidence for either. More likely, it was simply the result of an expansion through, and an exploitation of, what previously had been unsettled farming territory. The first architectural signs of a nonegalitarian condition are almost concomitant with, or follow immediately upon, this population expansion. The Altar de Sacrificios community now becomes organized around a ceremonial or politico-religious center. Certain individuals, presumably leaders, are given special, honored burial in the buildings of such a center. There is a development of luxury craft goods, along with the importation of both manufactured and raw material exotics. Monumental art and the stela cult followed a bit later.

I think that all of this is especially revealing as to the origins of what we call Classic Maya civilization. This civilization partook of elements that were not indigenous to it, but the dynamics of its development on the lowland scene were essentially local; that is, Maya civilization was not introduced to the lowlands as an intact, fully organized cultural system. To be sure, the idea of ceremonial-center construction (and the condition of a nonegalitarian society which it implies) was known earlier in the neighboring highlands, and the lowland settlers were undoubtedly familiar with these features and institutions from their contacts with the highlanders; but the processes of population growth and the necessity for the organization of these increased populations were *in situ* lowland phenomena, generated at Altar de Sacrificios and elsewhere in the lowlands. These processes, insofar as we can isolate "triggering" action, were the things that touched off the crucial transition from simple-to-complex society in the lowlands. Only when this complex social base had been provided at Altar de Sacrificios and elsewhere in the lowlands were still other new ideas in ceramics and monumental art accepted and refashioned into parts of the newly emerging cultural system known as Classic Maya civilization.

While this analysis has focused on Altar de Sacrificios and the lower Pasión, we know that other southern lowland sites and regions were undergoing very similar changes at about the same time. Indeed, in the northeast Peten, at Uaxactun and Tikal, such processes leading to a complex social order had probably begun somewhat ahead of those at Altar. Certainly, the archaeological records (see A. L. Smith 1950; W. R. Coe 1965) from these sites show that the crucial quantum jump from simple-to-complex society had taken place in the Late Preclassic Period, or well prior to the first appearances of Maya style polychrome ceramics or carved stelae. In other words, the interpretation offered here, in this attempt to elucidate process, sees the southern Maya lowlands of Middle to Late Preclassic times as characterized by a general social evolution—one linked systemically to numerous localized subsistence successes and population increases. And only after this evolution had taken place did the emergent nonegalitarian societies assimilate other traits compatible with such a social structure, borrowing from the then somewhat more advanced highland cultures the seed ideas that were to flourish in the lowland Classic stela cult and luxury craft goods traditions. While such ideas may have been implanted first in the northeast Peten, as the record for monumental carving, hieroglyphics, and long-count calendrics seems now to indicate, their diffusion to other centers in the lowlands always rode upon, and was received into, a prepared complex social structural base.

This, in any event, is the best general interpretation I can come up with for the rise of

Altar de Sacrificios and for the initial development of Maya lowland civilization as a whole. It is a sketchy outline, a pointing toward an understanding of process, as I have said, rather than an achievement of it. I realize that my opening statement or question, that Maya society changed from an egalitarian to a nonegalitarian one, is really more of a broad historical proposition than a specific hypothesis. The data for its answer, and even the answer, are fairly self-evident at the outset so that there is a certain circularity to the argument. The more complex questions that remain before us are those pertaining to the causal interplay of factors that brought about this change. At Altar de Sacrificios I think we have made some steps in beginning to sort out internal versus diffusional factors in the long Preclassic-to-Classic transformation; but, again, I emphasize that this is only a start.

Certainly, a great many hypotheses and tests could be devised within this general framework of the egalitarian-to-nonegalitarian inquiry. My Altar de Sacrificios colleague Adams (1970) has made one start in this direction by his examination of the question of occupational specialization in the Maya lowlands. Marshall Becker (1972) has followed this up at Tikal, and a number of other young archaeologists are concerned with this question. I only regret that the Altar data were not more suitably excavated and recorded with this occupational specialization problem in mind. In another direction, Haviland, among his several innovative papers on Tikal, has devoted one to changes in kin group organization, the probable relationships of this to land control, and of all of this to the broader gamut of the change from simple-to-complex (Haviland 1966). Still another, and a highly productive line of investigation, is that pioneered by Rathje in which he has systematically combined burial placement and grave goods, regional resources, and trading patterns to provide a series of hypotheses and tests concerning changes in social mobility and class structure through time (Rathje 1970, 1971a and b, 1973). Happily, in this attempt, Rathje was able to draw upon some of the Altar de Sacrificios data presented here and in the series of reports which back up this summary and concluding statement.

APPENDIX

ERRATA OR DISCREPANCIES IN DESIGNATIONS IN PREVIOUS ALTAR DE SACRIFICIOS MONOGRAPHS

In the preparation of this summary, after the completion of all of the other Altar de Sacrificios monographs, several differences and discrepancies between volumes came to light. Some of these were matters of differing judgment and opinions between authors, such as the minor differences in dating estimates between Adams (1971) and Smith (1972), or comments on human skeletal materials between Smith (1972) and Saul (1972). These have been referred to in the text or footnotes of this summary. In these particular instances, the Adams-Smith chronological estimate differences have simply been listed and explained. The Smith-Saul differences in observations on skeletal materials have been indicated as being resolved in the favor of Saul, the physical anthropologist whose laboratory examinations of the materials in question take precedence over Smith's archaeological field observations.

There have also been some errors in some monographs on monument designations, and map position of monuments. Most of these have been referred to in this summary and corrected. There remain a few others:

On page 160 of Adams (1971), the reference to Stela 21 at the end of the second paragraph on that page should actually be a reference to the monument Plain Altar 18.

In Adams's table on Ceramics in House Mounds (Adams 1971, table 21, p. 108) there are some other errors or discrepancies in designation, occasioned, for the most part, by some changes made in field designations during the course of the work at Altar. These may be summarized as follows:

Op. 92 (House Mound 105). There is no such house mound in our tabulations. Op. 92 was a pit excavated just east of Structure B-IV. It may have gone into a buried house mound feature, however.

Op. 93 (House Mound A-6). There is no such house mound in our tabulations. Op. 93 was a test excavation in a little court bounded by Structures A-I, A-VII, and A-VIII.

Op. 100 (House Mound C-I). Again, there is no such formal designation for a house mound. Structure C-I was a part of C Group. However, it was a small structure, and its functions may have been comparable to those of the formal House Mound series.

Op. 83 (House Mound 29). This is a typographical or clerical error. Op. 83 is associated with House Mound 20.

Op. 103 (House Mound C-4). House Mound C-4, or C-IV should be House Mound 41.

Four other House Mounds, Nos. 1 (Ops. 22 and 105), 2 (Ops. 38 and 46), 13 (Op. 108), and 40 (Op. 104) are not listed on the table.

While we are at pains to set the record straight on all of these matters, we do not feel that they have any very crucial bearings on the nature of our results at, or conclusions about, Altar de Sacrificios.

BIBLIOGRAPHY

Adams, R. E. W.

1969. "Maya Archaeology 1958–1968, A Review," *Latin American Research Review,* vol. 4, no. 2, pp. 3–45.

1970. "Suggested Classic Period Occupational Specialization in the Southern Maya Lowlands," *Monographs and Papers in Maya Archaeology,* W. R. Bullard, editor, pp. 487–502. Papers of the Peabody Museum, Harvard University, vol. 61, Cambridge, Massachusetts.

1971. *The Ceramics of Altar de Sacrificios.* Papers of the Peabody Museum, Harvard University, vol. 63, no. 1, Cambridge, Massachusetts.

1973. "Maya Collapse: Transformation and Termination in the Ceramic Sequence at Altar de Sacrificios," in *The Collapse of Ancient Maya Civilization: A New Assessment,* T. P. Culbert, editor. School of American Research, Santa Fe, New Mexico.

Andrews, E. W., IV

1960. "Excavations at Dzibilchaltun, Northwestern Yucatan, Mexico," *Proceedings of the American Philosophical Society,* vol. 104, no. 3, Philadelphia, Pennsylvania.

1971. "The Emergence of Civilization in the Maya Lowlands," *Observations on the Emergence of Civilization in Mesoamerica,* R. F. Heizer and J. A. Graham, editors, pp. 85–97. Contributions of the University of California Archaeological Research Facility, no. 11, Berkeley.

Becker, M. J.

1972. "Archaeological Evidence for Occupational Specialization Among the Classic Period Maya at Tikal, Guatemala." Mimeographed.

Berger, Rainer, J. A. Graham, and R. F. Heizer

1967. "A Reconsideration of the Age of the La Venta Site," *Studies in Olmec Archaeology.* Contributions of the University of California Archaeological Research Facility, no. 3, pp. 1–24, Berkeley.

Berlin, Heinrich

1956. *Late Pottery Horizons of Tabasco, Mexico.* Carnegie Institution of Washington, Publication no. 606, Contributions to American Anthropology and History, no. 59, Washington, D.C.

Binford, L. R.

1968. "Some Comments on Historical Versus Processual Archaeology," *Southwestern Journal of Anthropology,* vol. 24, no. 3, pp. 267–275, Albuquerque, New Mexico.

Borhegyi, S. F. de

1963. "Pre-Columbian Pottery Mushrooms from Mesoamerica," *American Antiquity,* vol. 28, no. 3, pp. 328–338, Salt Lake City, Utah.

1965. "Archaeological Synthesis of the Guatemalan Highlands," *Handbook of Middle American Indians,* vol. 2, Archaeology of Southern Mesoamerica, part I, Robert Wauchope and G. R. Willey, editors, pp. 3–59. University of Texas Press, Austin.

Brainerd, G. W.

1958. *The Archaeological Ceramics of Yucatan.* Anthropological Records, no. 19, University of California Press, Berkeley and Los Angeles.

Bullard, W. R. Jr.

1960. "The Maya Settlement Pattern in Northeastern Peten, Guatemala," *American Antiquity,* vol. 25, pp. 355–372, Salt Lake City, Utah.

1970. "Topoxte: A Postclassic Maya Site in Peten, Guatemala," *Monographs and Papers in Maya Archaeology,* W. R. Bullard, Jr., editor, pp. 245–307. Papers of the Peabody Museum, Harvard University, vol. 61, Cambridge, Massachusetts.

1973. "Postclassic Culture in Central Peten and Adjacent British Honduras," in *The Collapse of Ancient Maya Civilization: A New Assessment,* T. P. Culbert, editor. School of American Research, Santa Fe, New Mexico.

Butler, Mary

1935a. "A Study of Maya Mould-made Figurines," *American Anthropologist,* vol. 37, no. 4, pp. 636–672, Menasha, Wisconsin.

1935b. "Piedras Negras Pottery," *Piedras Negras Preliminary Papers,* no. 4, The University Museum, University of Pennsylvania, Philadelphia.

1940. "A Pottery Sequence from the Alta Verapaz, Guatemala," in *The Maya and Their Neighbors,* C. L. Hay and others, editors. New York, New York.

Coe, M. D.

1961. *La Victoria, an Early Site on the Pacific Coast of Guatemala.* Papers of the Peabody Museum, Harvard University, vol. 53, Cambridge, Massachusetts.

1968. "San Lorenzo and the Olmec Civilization,"

Dumbarton Oaks Conference on the Olmec, October 28th and 29th, 1967, E. Benson, editor, pp. 41–78, Dumbarton Oaks, Washington, D.C.

Coe, M. D. and K. V. Flannery

1967. *Early Cultures and Human Ecology in South Coastal Guatemala,* Smithsonian Institution, Contributions to Anthropology, vol. 3, Washington, D.C.

Coe, W. R.

1962. "A Summary of Excavation and Research at Tikal, Guatemala: 1956–1961," *American Antiquity,* vol. 27, no. 4, pp. 479–507. Salt Lake City, Utah.

1965. "Tikal: Ten Years of Study of a Maya Ruin in the Lowlands of Guatemala," *Expedition,* vol. 8, no. 1, pp. 5–56, The University Museum, University of Pennsylvania, Philadelphia.

1967. *Tikal, A Handbook of the Ancient Maya Ruins.* The University Museum, University of Pennsylvania, Philadelphia.

Cowgill, G. L.

1963. "Postclassic Period Culture in the Vicinity of Flores, Peten, Guatemala," Ph.D. dissertation, Department of Anthropology, Harvard University, Cambridge, Massachusetts.

Culbert, T. P.

1973. "The Maya Downfall at Tikal, Guatemala," in *The Collapse of Ancient Maya Civilization: A New Assessment,* T. P. Culbert, editor. School of American Research, Santa Fe, New Mexico.

Culbert, T. P., editor

1973. *The Collapse of Ancient Maya Civilization: A New Assessment.* School of American Research, Santa Fe, New Mexico.

Dixon, K. A.

1959. *Ceramics from Two Preclassic Periods at Chiapa de Corzo, Southern Mexico.* Papers of the New World Archaeological Foundation, no. 5, Publication no. 4, Orinda, California.

Drucker, Philip

1943a. *Ceramic Sequences at Tres Zapotes, Veracruz, Mexico.* Bureau of American Ethnology, Bulletin 140, Smithsonian Institution, Washington, D.C.

1943b. *Ceramic Stratigraphy at Cerro de las Mesas, Veracruz, Mexico.* Bureau of American Ethnology, Bulletin 141, Smithsonian Institution, Washington, D.C.

Drucker, Philip, R. F. Heizer, and R. J. Squier

1959. *Excavations at La Venta, Tabasco, 1955.* Bureau of American Ethnology, Bulletin 170, Smithsonian Institution, Washington, D.C.

Flannery, K. V.

1968. "The Olmec and the Valley of Oaxaca: A Model for Inter-Regional Interaction in Formative Times," *Dumbarton Oaks Conference on the Olmec, October 28th and 29th, 1967,* E. Benson, editor, pp. 79–118, Dumbarton Oaks, Washington, D.C.

Gordon, G. B.

1896. *Prehistoric Ruins of Copan, Honduras.* Memoirs of the Peabody Museum, Harvard University, vol. 1, no. 1, Cambridge, Massachusetts.

Graham, J. A.

1972a. *The Hieroglyphic Inscriptions and Monumental Art of Altar de Sacrificios.* Papers of the Peabody Museum, Harvard University, vol. 64, no. 2, Cambridge, Massachusetts.

1972b. "Some Final Moments of Lowland Classic Maya Art," in *Tulane Studies in the History of Art,* vol. 1, in preparation. Tulane University, New Orleans, Louisiana.

1973. "Aspects of Non-Classic Presences in the Sculpture and Epigraphy of Seibal," in *The Collapse of Ancient Maya Civilization: A New Assessment,* T. P. Culbert, editor. School of American Research, Santa Fe, New Mexico.

Graham, J. A. and Howel Williams

1971. "Two Unusual Maya Stelae," *Papers on Olmec and Maya Archaeology.* Contributions of the University of California Archaeological Research Facility, no. 13, Berkeley.

Green, D. F. and G. W. Lowe

1967. *Altamira and Padre Piedra, Early Preclassic Sites in Chiapas, Mexico.* Papers of the New World Archaeological Foundation, no. 20, Publication no. 15, Brigham Young University, Provo, Utah.

Gruning, E. L.

1930. "Report on the British Museum Expedition to British Honduras, 1930," *Journal of the Royal Anthropological Institute,* vol. 60, pp. 477–483, London.

Hammond, Norman

1970. "Excavations at Lubaantun, 1970," *Antiquity,* vol. 44, no. 175, pp. 216–223, Cambridge, England.

Haviland, W. A.

1966. "Social Integration and the Classic Maya," *American Antiquity,* vol. 31, no. 5, part 1, pp. 625–632, Salt Lake City, Utah.

Heizer, R. F.

1968. "New Observations on La Venta," *Dumbarton Oaks Conference on the Olmec, October 28th and 29th, 1967,* E. Benson, editor, pp. 9–40, Dumbarton Oaks, Washington, D.C.

JOESINK-MANDEVILLE, L. R. V.
1971. "The Olmec Gulf Coast Region and Northwestern Yucatan During the Middle Formative." Mimeographed.

JOYCE, T. A.
1926. "Report on the Investigations at Lubaantun, British Honduras, in 1926," *Journal of the Royal Anthropological Institute*, vol. 56, pp. 208–230, London.
1933. "The Pottery Whistle-Figurines of Lubaantun," *Journal of the Royal Anthropological Institute*, vol. 63, pp. xv–xxv, London.

KIDDER, A. V., J. D. JENNINGS, AND E. M. SHOOK
1946. *Excavations at Kaminaljuyu, Guatemala.* Carnegie Institution of Washington, Publication no. 561, Washington, D.C.

LEE, T. A., JR.
1969. *The Artifacts of Chiapa de Corzo, Chiapas, Mexico.* Papers of the New World Archaeological Foundation, no. 26, Brigham Young University, Provo, Utah.

LONGYEAR, J. M., III
1952. *Copan Ceramics: A Study of Southeastern Maya Pottery*. Carnegie Institution of Washington, Publication no. 597, Washington, D.C.

LOTHROP, S. K.
1924. *Tulum.* Carnegie Institution of Washington, Publication no. 335, Washington, D.C.

MACNEISH, R. S.
1954. *An Early Archaeological Site near Panuco, Veracruz.* Transactions of the American Philosophical Society, vol. 44, pt. 5, Philadelphia, Pennsylvania.
1967. "Introduction," *The Prehistory of the Tehuacan Valley, Vol. One: Environment and Subsistence*, D. S. Byers, editor, pp. 3–13, R. S. Peabody Foundation, Andover, Massachusetts and University of Texas Press, Austin.

MACNEISH, R. S. AND F. A. PETERSON
1962. *The Santa Marta Rock Shelter, Ocozocoautla, Chiapas, Mexico.* Papers of the New World Archaeological Foundation, no. 14, Brigham Young University, Provo, Utah.

MACNEISH, R. S., F. A. PETERSON, AND K. V. FLANNERY
1970. *Ceramics. The Prehistory of the Tehuacan Valley*, vol. 3. University of Texas Press, Austin.

MALER, TEOBERT
1908. *Explorations of the Upper Usumatsintla and Adjacent Region.* Memoirs of the Peabody Museum, Harvard University, vol. 4, no. 1, Cambridge, Massachusetts.

MAUDSLAY, A. P.
1883. "Explorations in Guatemala and Examination of the Newly-Discovered Ruins of Quirigua, Tikal, and the Usumacinta," *Proceedings of the Royal Geographical Society*, vol. 5, pp. 185–204, London.

MERWIN, R. E. AND G. C. VAILLANT
1932. *The Ruins of Holmul, Guatemala.* Memoirs of the Peabody Museum, Harvard University, vol. 3, no. 2, Cambridge, Massachusetts.

MILES, S. W.
1965. "Sculpture of the Guatemala-Chiapas Highlands and Pacific Slopes, and Associated Hieroglyphs," *Handbook of Middle American Indians, vol. 2, Archaeology of Southern Mesoamerica*, part I, Robert Wauchope and G. R. Willey, editors, pp. 237–276. University of Texas Press, Austin.

MORLEY, S. G.
1920. *The Inscriptions at Copan.* Carnegie Institution of Washington, Publication no. 219, Washington, D.C.
1937–38. *The Inscriptions of Peten.* Carnegie Institution of Washington, Publication no. 437, 5 vols., Washington, D.C.

MORRIS, E. H., JEAN CHARLOT, AND A. A. MORRIS
1931. *The Temple of the Warriors at Chichen Itza, Yucatan.* Carnegie Institution of Washington, Publication no. 406, Washington, D.C.

NAVARRETE, CARLOS
1960. *Archaeological Explorations in the Region of the Frailesca, Chiapas, Mexico.* Papers of the New World Archaeological Foundation, no. 7, Publication no. 6, Orinda, California.

PETERSON, F. A.
1963. *Some Ceramics from Mirador, Chiapas, Mexico.* Papers of the New World Archaeological Foundation, no. 15, Publication no. 11, Brigham Young University, Provo, Utah.

POLLOCK, H. E. D.
1970. "Architectural Notes on Some Chenes Ruins," *Monographs and Papers in Maya Archaeology*, W. R. Bullard, editor, pp. 1–87. Papers of the Peabody Museum, Harvard University, vol. 61, Cambridge, Massachusetts.

POLLOCK, H. E. D., R. L. ROYS, T. PROSKOURIAKOFF, AND A. L. SMITH
1962. *Mayapan, Yucatan, Mexico.* Carnegie Institution of Washington, Publication no. 619, Washington, D.C.

PROSKOURIAKOFF, TATIANA
1950. *A Study of Classic Maya Sculpture.* Carnegie Institution of Washington, Publication no. 593, Washington, D.C.

PULESTON, D. E. AND O. S. PULESTON
1971. "An Ecological Approach to the Origins of

Maya Civilization," *Archaeology*, vol. 24, no. 4, pp. 330–337, New York, New York.

RANDS, ROBERT

1973. "Chronological Summary," (a tentative title), in *The Collapse of Ancient Maya Civilization: A New Assessment*, T. P. Culbert, editor. School of American Research, Santa Fe, New Mexico.

RATHJE, W. L.

1970. "Socio-political Implications of Lowland Maya Burials: Methodology and Tentative Hypotheses," *World Archaeology*, vol. I, no. 3, pp. 359–375, London.

1971a. "The Origin and Development of Lowland Classic Maya Civilization," *American Antiquity*, vol. 36, no. 3, pp. 275–286, Salt Lake City, Utah.

1971b. "Lowland Classic Maya Socio-Political Organization: Degree and Form Through Time and Space," Ph.D. dissertation, Department of Anthropology, Harvard University.

1973. "Classic Maya Development and Denouement," in *The Collapse of Ancient Maya Civilization: A New Assessment*, T. P. Culbert, editor. School of American Research, Santa Fe, New Mexico.

RICKETSON, O. G., JR. AND E. B. RICKETSON

1937. *Uaxactun, Guatemala, Group E–1926–1931*. Carnegie Institution of Washington, Publication no. 477, Washington, D.C.

ROWE, J. H.

1960. "Cultural Unity and Diversification in Peruvian Archaeology," *Men and Cultures*. Selected Papers, 5th International Congress of Anthropological and Ethnological Sciences, A. F. C. Wallace, editor, pp. 627–631. University of Pennsylvania Press, Philadelphia.

RUPPERT, KARL

1935. *The Caracol at Chichen Itza, Yucatan, Mexico*. Carnegie Institution of Washington, Publication no. 454, Washington, D.C.

RUPPERT, KARL, J. E. S. THOMPSON, AND TATIANA PROSKOURIAKOFF

1955. *Bonampak, Chiapas, Mexico*. Carnegie Institution of Washington, Publication no. 602, Washington, D.C.

RUZ LHUILLIER, ALBERTO

1952a. "Exploraciones arqueológicas en Palenque: 1949," *Anales*, Instituto de Antropología e Historia, vol. 4, pp. 49–60. Secretaria de Educación Pública, Mexico, D.F.

1952b. "Exploraciones en Palenque: 1950 and 1951," *Anales*, Instituto de Antropología e Historia, vol. 5, pp. 25–66. Secretaria de Educación Pública, Mexico, D.F.

1958. "Exploraciones arqueológicas en Palenque: 1953–1956, *Anales*, Instituto Nacional de Antropología e Historia, vol. 10, pp. 69–299. Secretaria de Educación Pública, Mexico, D.F.

1962. "Exploraciones en Palenque: 1957 and 1958," *Anales*, Instituto Nacional de Antropología e Historia, vol. 14, pp. 35–120. Secretaria de Educación Pública, Mexico, D.F.

SABLOFF, J. A.

1970. "Type Descriptions of the Fine Paste Ceramics of the Bayal Boca Complex, Seibal, Peten, Guatemala," *Monographs and Papers in Maya Archaeology*, W. R. Bullard, editor, pp. 357–404. Papers of the Peabody Museum, Harvard University, vol. 61, Cambridge, Massachusetts.

1971. "Review of *Maya History and Religion* by J. E. S. Thompson," *American Anthropologist*, vol. 73, no. 4, pp. 915–916, Menasha, Wisconsin.

1973. "Continuity and Disruption During Terminal Late Classic Times at Seibal: Ceramic and Other Evidence," *The Collapse of Ancient Maya Civilization: A New Assessment*, T. P. Culbert, editor. School of American Research, Santa Fe, New Mexico.

SABLOFF, J. A. AND G. R. WILLEY

1967. "The Collapse of Maya Civilization in the Southern Lowlands: A Consideration of History and Process," *Southwestern Journal of Anthropology*, vol. 23, no. 4, pp. 311–336, University of New Mexico, Albuquerque.

SANDERS, W. T.

1960. *Prehistoric Ceramics and Settlement Patterns in Quintana Roo, Mexico*. Carnegie Institution of Washington, Publication no. 606, Contributions to American Anthropology and History, vol. 12, no. 60, pp. 155–264, Washington, D.C.

1961. *Ceramic Stratigraphy at Santa Cruz, Chiapas, Mexico*. Papers of the New World Archaeological Foundation, no. 13, Provo, Utah.

SATTERTHWAITE, LINTON, JR.

1933. *Description of the Site (Piedras Negras) with Short Notes on the Excavations of 1931–32*. Piedras Negras Preliminary Papers, no. 1, The University Museum, Philadelphia, Pennsylvania.

1936. "Notes on the Work of the Fourth and Fifth University Museum Expeditions to Piedras Negras, Petén, Guatemala," *Maya Research*, vol. 3, no. 1, pp. 1–18, New Orleans, Louisiana.

SAUL, F. P.

1972. *The Human Skeletal Remains of Altar de Sacrificios. An Osteobiographical Analysis*. Papers of the Peabody Museum, Harvard

University, vol. 63, no. 2, Cambridge, Massachusetts.

SAYRE, E. V., L.-H. CHAN, AND J. A. SABLOFF
1971. "High Resolution Gamma Ray Spectroscopic Analysis of Mayan Fine Orange Pottery," *Science and Archaeology*, R. Brill, editor, M.I.T. Press, Cambridge, Massachusetts.

SCHOLES, F. V. AND R. L. ROYS
1948. *The Maya Chontal Indians of Acalan-Tixchel*. Carnegie Institution of Washington, Publication no. 560, Washington, D.C.

SEDAT, D. W.
1972. "The Preclassic Lowland Maya and Their Northern Highland Neighbors." Mimeographed. Paper read before the thirty-seventh annual meeting of the Society for American Archaeology, May 5, Bal Harbour, Florida.

SEDAT, D. W. AND R. J. SHARER
1972. "Archaeological Investigations in the Northern Maya Highlands: New Data on the Maya Preclassic." Mimeographed.

SHARER, R. J. AND J. C. GIFFORD
1970. "Preclassic Ceramics from Chalchuapa, El Salvador, and their Relationships with the Maya Lowlands," *American Antiquity*, vol. 35, no. 4, pp. 441–462, Salt Lake City, Utah.

SHARER, R. J. AND D. W. SEDAT
1972. "New Evidence Concerning the Development of Maya Calendrical and Writing Systems." Xeroxed. Pitzer College, Claremont, California.

SHOOK, E. M.
1957. "The Tikal Project," *The University Museum Bulletin*, vol. 21, no. 3, pp. 36–52, The University Museum, University of Pennsylvania, Philadelphia.

SHOOK, E. M. AND A. V. KIDDER
1952. *Mound E–III–3, Kaminaljuyu, Guatemala*. Carnegie Institution of Washington, Publication no. 596, Contributions to American Anthropology and History, vol. 11, no. 53, Washington, D.C.

SMITH, A. L.
1950. *Uaxactun, Guatemala: Excavations of 1931–1937*. Carnegie Institution of Washington, Publication no. 588, Washington, D.C.
1955. *Archaeological Reconnaissance in Central Guatemala*. Carnegie Institution of Washington, Publication no. 608, Washington, D.C.
1972. *Excavations at Altar de Sacrificios: Architecture, Settlement, Burials, and Caches*. Papers of the Peabody Museum, Harvard University, vol. 62, no. 2, Cambridge, Massachusetts.

SMITH, A. L. AND A. V. KIDDER
1943. *Explorations in the Motagua Valley, Guatemala*. Carnegie Institution of Washington, Publication no. 546, Contributions to American Anthropology and History, vol. 8, no. 41, Washington, D.C.
1951. *Excavations at Nebaj, Guatemala*. Carnegie Institution of Washington, Publication no. 594, Washington, D.C.

SMITH, A. L. AND G. R. WILLEY
1962. "Preliminary Report on Excavations at Altar de Sacrificios, 1959–1960," *Proceedings*, 34th International Congress of Americanists, Vienna, pp. 318–325.
1969. "Seibal, Guatemala, in 1968: A Brief Summary of Archaeological Results," *38th International Congress of Americanists*, vol. 1, pp. 151–157, Stuttgart-Munich.

SMITH, R. E.
1955. *Ceramic Sequence at Uaxactun, Guatemala*, 2 vols. Middle American Research Institute, Tulane University, Publication no. 20, New Orleans, Louisiana.
1958. "The Place of Fine Orange Pottery in Mesoamerican Archaeology," *American Antiquity*, vol. 24, no. 2, pp. 151–160, Salt Lake City, Utah.

SMITH, R. E. AND J. C. GIFFORD
1965. "Pottery of the Maya Lowlands," *Handbook of Middle American Indians*, vol. 2, *Archaeology of Southern Mesoamerica*, part I, R. Wauchope and G. R. Willey, editors, pp. 498–534. University of Texas Press, Austin.
1966. *Maya Ceramic Varieties, Types, and Wares at Uaxactun: Supplement to "Ceramic Sequence at Uaxactun, Guatemala."* Middle American Research Institute, Publication no. 28, pp. 125–174, Tulane University, New Orleans, Louisiana.

SPINDEN, H. J.
1913. *A Study of Maya Art, Its Subject Matter and Historical Development*. Memoirs of the Peabody Museum, Harvard University, vol. 6, Cambridge, Massachusetts.

THOMPSON, J. E. S.
1931. *Archaeological Investigations in the Southern Cayo District, British Honduras*. Field Museum of Natural History, Anthropological Series, vol. 17, no. 3. Chicago, Illinois.
1939. *Excavations at San Jose, British Honduras*. Carnegie Institution of Washington, Publication no. 506, Washington, D.C.
1943. "A Trial Survey of the Southern Maya Area," *American Antiquity*, vol. 9, pp. 106–134, Menasha, Wisconsin.
1945. "A Survey of the Northern Maya Area," *American Antiquity*, vol. 11, pp. 2–24, Menasha, Wisconsin.

1951. "The Itzá of Tayasal, Peten," *Homenaje al Doctor Alfonso Caso*, pp. 389–400, Mexico, D.F.

1970. *Maya History and Religion.* University of Oklahoma Press, Norman.

TOLSTOY, PAUL AND L. I. PARADIS

1971. "Early and Middle Preclassic Culture in the Basin of Mexico," *Observations on the Emergence of Civilization in Mesoamerica*, R. F. Heizer and J. A. Graham, editors, pp. 7–29. Contributions of the University of California Archaeological Research Facility, no. 11, Berkeley.

WARREN, B. W.

1961. "The Archaeological Sequence at Chiapa de Corzo," in Sociedad Mexicana de Antropología, 8th Mesa Redonda, *Los Mayas del Sur y sus Relaciones con los Nahuas Meridionales*, pp. 75–83, Mexico, D.F.

WAUCHOPE, ROBERT

1948. *Excavations at Zacualpa, Guatemala.* Middle American Research Institute, Publication no. 14, Tulane University, New Orleans, Louisiana.

WEBB, M. C.

1964. "The Post-Classic Decline of the Peten Maya: An Interpretation in the Light of a General Theory of State Society," Ph.D. dissertation. Facsimile, Department of Anthropology, University of Michigan, Ann Arbor.

1973. "The Peten Maya Decline Viewed in the Perspective of State Formation," *The Collapse of Ancient Maya Civilization: A New Assessment*, T. P. Culbert, editor. School of American Research, Santa Fe, New Mexico.

WILLEY, G. R.

1966. *An Introduction to American Archaeology: vol. I. North and Middle America.* Prentice-Hall, Inc., Englewood Cliffs, New Jersey.

1970. "Type Descriptions of the Ceramics of the Real Xe Complex, Seibal, Peten, Guatemala," *Monographs and Papers in Maya Archaeology*, W. R. Bullard, editor, pp. 313–357. Papers of the Peabody Museum, Harvard University, vol. 61, Cambridge, Massachusetts.

1972. *The Artifacts of Altar de Sacrificios.* Papers of the Peabody Museum, Harvard University, vol. 64, no. 1, Cambridge, Massachusetts.

1973. "The Classic Maya Hiatus: A 'Rehearsal' for the Collapse." Manuscript prepared for a symposium on Mesoamerican archaeology, Cambridge, England, August 1972.

WILLEY, G. R. AND W. R. BULLARD, JR.

1961. "Altar de Sacrificios, Guatemala: Mapa Preliminar y Resumen de Las Excavaciones," *Estudios de Cultura Maya*, vol. 1, pp. 81–86, Universidad Autonoma de Mexico, D.F.

1965. "Prehistoric Settlement Patterns in the Maya Lowlands," *Handbook of Middle American Indians*, vol. 2, *Archaeology of Southern Mesoamerica*, part I, Robert Wauchope and G. R. Willey, editors, pp. 360–378. University of Texas Press, Austin.

WILLEY, G. R., W. R. BULLARD, JR., J. B. GLASS, AND J. C. GIFFORD

1965. *Prehistoric Maya Settlements in the Belize Valley*, Papers of the Peabody Museum, Harvard University, vol. 54, Cambridge, Massachusetts.

WILLEY, G. R., T. P. CULBERT, AND R. E. W. ADAMS, EDITORS

1967. "Maya Lowland Ceramics: A Report from the 1965 Guatemala City Conference," *American Antiquity*, vol. 32, no. 3, pp. 289–316, Salt Lake City, Utah.

WILLEY, G. R. AND J. C. GIFFORD

1961. "Pottery of the Holmul I Style from Barton Ramie, British Honduras," in *Essays in Pre-Columbian Art and Archaeology*, S. K. Lothrop and others, pp. 152–170.

WILLEY, G. R. AND D. B. SHIMKIN

1971. "The Collapse of Classic Maya Civilization in the Southern Lowlands: A Symposium Summary Statement," *Southwestern Journal of Anthropology*, vol. 27, pp. 1–18, University of New Mexico, Albuquerque.

1973. "The Maya Collapse: A Summary View," in *The Collapse of Ancient Maya Civilization: A New Assessment*, T. P. Culbert, editor. School of American Research, Santa Fe, New Mexico.

WILLEY, G. R. AND A. L. SMITH

1963. "New Discoveries at Altar de Sacrificios, Guatemala," *Archaeology*, vol. 16, no. 2, pp. 83–89, Cambridge, Massachusetts.

1967. "A Temple at Seibal, Guatemala," *Archaeology*, vol. 20, no. 4, pp. 290–299, Cambridge, Massachusetts.

1969. *The Ruins of Altar de Sacrificios, Department of Peten, Guatemala, An Introduction.* Papers of the Peabody Museum, Harvard University, vol. 62, no. 1, Cambridge, Massachusetts.

WILLEY, G. R., A. L. SMITH, W. R. BULLARD, JR., AND J. A. GRAHAM

1960. "Altar de Sacrificios, a Prehistoric Maya Crossroads," *Archaeology*, vol. 13, pp. 110–117, Cambridge, Massachusetts.